the
upside
uʍop
marriage

To Hed + Betty:

God's blessings!

[signature]

[praise for upside down marriage]

"I have known Jim for many years and have always appreciated his insights on living life and having a rich family experience."

Steve Douglass
President and Chairman, Campus Crusade for Christ

"Jim Keller's wife, Renee, is one of my best friends. I have seen their marriage for years—our girls played soccer together. Here's what I love about Jim: He believes in his wife. Renee is gifted and smart and capable and so energetic. And Jim loves her and encourages her and helps her and believes in her—to be all that God created her to be. That's how I know Jim knows what works for a good marriage—he has lived it out."

Judy Douglass
Writer, Speaker, Director of Women's Resources at
Campus Crusade for Christ

"Jim Keller is wise and insightful. This book is full of practical, biblical, and helpful admonitions that challenge conventional wisdom and offer a better way to live. Reading this won't make your marriage better, but it will give you some new tools to do the work and again new perspective on your relationship."

Isaac Hunter
Senior Pastor of Summit Church, Orlando, Florida

"Jim Keller's upside-down perspective on marriage makes more sense than any right-side-up approach we've seen in a long time! This book represents the accumulated wisdom of thousands of hours of Jim's counseling experience in a creative and practical form. It's like free marriage counseling with Jim!"

Tim and Joy Downs
Authors of *Fight Fair* and *One of Us Must Be Crazy*

"When we had a friend who was in marital crisis the first person we thought of was Jim. His insight and compassion helped stabilize and recover their marriage. When we have our own questions about parenting or marriage, Jim is our most valued resource. The highest endorsement I can give is to say we trust him with our relationship and those of our friends."

Tim Muehlhoff, Ph.D.
Associate Professor of Communication, Biola University.
Author of *Marriage Forecasting*

"I have been a long-time fan and disciple of Jim Keller. He has a refreshing blend of honesty, irreverence for the status quo, reverence for God, and sharp wit—not to mention this penchant for a catchy turn of phrase—all of which make him easy, engaging, fun, and challenging to read. Any couple, whether newlyweds preparing for a marriage (rather than a wedding) or «oldlyweds» looking to improve their relationship, will learn from reading Jim›s practical and off-beat words of wisdom."

Pamela Cochran
Visiting Asst. Professor of Religion
Coordinator, Center on Religion and Environment, University of Virginia

"Having known Jim for almost forty years, I am not surprised by his thought provoking, thoroughly biblical, wise and practical book. Drawing from over two decades of experience as a marriage counselor as well as his personal experience as a husband and father, Jim has taken a familiar topic—improving your marriage—and literally turned the conversation upside down, giving each reader a fresh and enlightening angle on the marriage relationship. Jim has a winsome way of speaking the truth in love, providing readers with candid insights, powerful illustrations and a good dose of humor. This book is a joy to read!"

Mark McCloskey, Ph.D
Program Director, M.A. in Transformational Leadership, Bethel Seminary

the
upside
uʍop
marriage

[12 Ways to Keep Your Marriage **Right** Side Up]

JIM KELLER

RM RUSSELL MEDIA

Boise, Idaho

Copyright © 2012 by James Mark Keller

Editorial Work by Chris Keller

Published in Boise, Idaho by Russell Media

Web: http://www.russell-media.com

For information please email info@russell-media.com.

ISBN (print): 978-1-937-498-115

ISBN (e-book): 978-1-937-498-122

Cover and Text Design by Woohoo Ink, LLC

Printed in the United States of America

This book may be purchased in bulk for educational, business, ministry, or promotional use.

[contents]

I find it more than just a little interesting that we enter into a lifelong commitment, called marriage, with such little preparation. As a young man I took drivers ed one summer; I read and re-read a driver's safety manual and practiced driving for months with my dad on gravel roads. THEN I had to take a written exam and prove I could actually drive with an officer seated in the passenger seat....just so I could get a license and learn how to really drive a car. The entire process is etched in my memory.

When Barbara and I married back in September of 1972 I can't even recall a single thing about what it took to get a marriage license. We have a license, so I must have gone to the courthouse and bought one. I DO recall the ceremony, but there were no tests, no instructors, and little if any preparation. And for sure, there were no coaches, mentors or role models who made the journey with us in our first months of marriage. I think we may have repeated our "rookie" season two years in a row.

Is it any wonder why marriages end up, so average? Why so many fail?

After the ceremony, we ALL need help. That's why I thank God for my friend, Jim Keller.

Jim is not only one of the most talented counselors and therapists I know, but he is just a really good man who's effective at what he does. There are several key elements that contribute to Jim's effectiveness. I know that he says that he doesn't like lists, but I know that he'll forgive me because this list is about him!

First, he's a "no-baloney" man who listens well and has just the right words to coach others in the rugged journey of building an effective marriage. It makes it easier to listen to what a professional has to say if you know he's the real deal. There's no veneer with Jim. He isn't perfect and you'll find that out right away as you read his book. He "connects" because he doesn't mind sharing what he's learned through his own failures.

Secondly, Jim is REALLY good as a counselor because his worldview is anchored in the bible and he has tens of thousands of hours of helping people. In short, he has a realistic understanding of people's needs and right expectations of what marriage is all about. He brings all kinds of stories of his experience of having journeyed through some deep valleys with all kinds of broken people.

Third, he loves people. You'll experience it and see it as you immerse yourself in these pages. He cares. It's not a soft, sentimental love, but a tough and tender mixture of truth and grace. He presents a plan that, if you can begin to practice it, you'll find that it really does work.

Next, Jim is appropriately irreverent—not of God, but of people. Where else could you find a book that tells you to "fight more", "have less sex", "go to church less", and "don't be such good parents." I have always liked the way he shakes people up and gets their attention. In person, Jim has a wry little smile that wrinkles its way across his face. You'll see that smile in every chapter. He shakes things up and gets your attention, then he doesn't leave you in a confused state, but puts the cookies out one at a time, so you'll enjoy them.

You REALLY are going to enjoy "The Upside Down Marriage." It's a fun read that's going to help you a lot!

Jim says he doesn't like lists…I'm not so sure about that.

Dennis Rainey
A friend of Jim
August 2012

[introduction]

Some years ago, some brilliant scientist solved the "ketchup problem." I grew up with glass ketchup bottles that simply refused to give up their red treasure easily. Pounding and prodding ketchup bottles was an art, but it seemed that the harder you tried to get that ketchup out, the more you failed. The solution? Build those bottles upside-down! You've seen them, the bottles are built to rest on a large plastic cap so the America's favorite condiment is ready to go at the first squeeze. The only problem I had initially in using these bottles was that I instinctively would place them in the refrigerator right-side up, and not on the intended large white cap. I forgot that the right way to place the bottle was "upside-down".

I came to the marriage counseling profession in mid-life. I was in my early forties and married over fifteen years, and I had already experienced many confusing paradoxes of marriage first hand. For me, marriage was a place of growth despite many times feeling as if I were failing as a husband. It seemed that despite my best efforts, the results of my actions were often the source of deep conflict. Often, what I thought was maturity was merely hubris, and what I assumed was failure often led, paradoxically, to places of deeper intimacy in our marriage. In other words, I've learned that the best way to love my wife is often paradoxical, inverted from my initial instincts, much like getting used to that new ketchup bottle.

As a marriage counselor, I have been privileged to walk through challenging relational dynamics with hundreds of couples. Sometime relationships rupture amidst life tragedies and heartbreaking betrayal. Other times, the slow erosion of passion and respect in the day-in-and-day-out challenges of marriage begins devoid of passion. Whether heartbreak or apathy has led a couple into my office, there always seems to be confusion about how things got so wrong, and confusion as to how to make things better. And many times we discover the "logical" answer isn't always clear; the better path to solutions is the "upside-down" path.

This book is about how to discover that inverted path to marital flourishing when our relational instincts have caused us to lose the plot. The goal of marriage is not to stay married; the goal of marriage is to flourish as a couple while simultaneously growing as individuals. The sum of the marriage is greater than the individual parts. Staying married is a natural by-product of two people growing together spiritually, emotionally, physically, and relationally. Couples who are happily married have a deep appreciation for the gift of marriage and what the commensurate lifetime commitment provides for personal and relational growth.

In order to illustrate the concept of the "upside-down marriage", I've included many stories in this book that have been culled from the tens of thousands of hours I've spent in marital therapy sessions. No story is taken directly from any one client, and every precaution has been made to protect the identity of real people. All the stories are based in truth, but they are composites and not actual situations. Therefore, any resemblance to actual individuals in these vignettes is purely circumstantial.

Finally, these chapters are mean to orient readers to their spouse in a new way, regardless of the age and health of the marriage, rather than produce a new set of rules to follow. Marriage is a place where our deepest insecurities and opportunities for growth are exposed, and therefore it is a place teeming with opportunities for healing, growth, and flourishing. I hope you will read this book with openness to learn about relationships, especially your own. And as you look at your own marriage through this different lens, may you move further toward a mutually caring marriage where you care for one another with humility and strength. So here's to remembering that what seems to be counterintuitive can many times lead us to a place of health and joy. Don't forget to turn the bottle onto its cap, it was designed to be "upside-down".

Jim Keller
Orlando, FL

chapter 1

don't talk so much

Everyone should be quick to listen, slow to speak, and slow to become angry.

JAMES 1:19 NIV

As I rose to greet Bill and Gail, it was easy to see that Bill was not pleased to be in a counseling office. As a freshly graduated and credentialed counselor, this was my first marriage counseling session on my own. Excited, and somewhat terrified, I began to conduct an intake with them. They had been married over thirty years, and as I heard more about the details of their relationship, it became obvious their relationship was in trouble.

Gail gave a thorough history of her marriage which ran, uninterrupted, for the first thirty minutes of the session. She had recently undergone radical surgery for breast cancer, and was one year into a difficult, but successful recovery. As her physical health improved, however, her emotional health was deteriorating. Gail's list of complaints about the marriage were really complaints about Bill. As she expounded on her grievances, her eyes welled up with tears, her voice shook with emotion. Her memories of Bill's failure were told carefully and critically.

Finally, it was Bill's turn to speak. Like a thunderclap out of a blue sky, Bill spoke his first words since the session started. "I don't know what her problem is! I don't abuse her. I don't drink too much. I earn a good living and support her." Then after pausing for breath, he repeated, "I don't know what her problem is." I was stunned. It seemed Bill hadn't heard a thing Gail had said in the last thirty minutes. She was nothing if not articulate, and I could have readily ticked off at least five issues that she had with Bill.

But lamentably, Bill had not heard a thing she said, and these were the only words that he uttered the entire fifty-minute session. Gail filled up the rest of the time with her genuine and heartfelt expressions of anger, grief, and disappointment.

The next appointment was a carbon copy of the first—Gail airing her complaints while Bill was silent, save for his similarly timed protest of, "I don't know what her problem is!" This cycle continued for three more sessions, until they decided to end their marriage counseling. At the time, I felt I was able to do some good for Gail but not for Bill. Bill never really got it; he was too defensive to address his personal and relational shortcomings.

About a decade later in a post-therapy analysis, I realized a simple truth that I totally missed at the time: Gail talked too much, and I had failed her by not helping her understand just that.

While this might seem like an awfully harsh thing to say about a woman who struggled for years with a dysfunctional marriage and a life-threatening illness, I did not help her communicate in a manner that Bill could hear. In retrospect, I should never have allowed a second session to go as the first, let alone five sessions of basically the same fare. It was not a good use of their time, or money for that matter.

* * * *

communication is the foundation of relationships

For several years I spoke at weekend conferences to help couples improve and grow in their marriages. The first message on communication had two main points: Listening and Expressing. I used to view this message as sort of a "Communication for Dummies" presentation. But as years went by and I absorbed more and more of what I was presenting, the importance of the presentation began to sink in. It was my practice during that message to make a statement that went like this: "There is nothing as easy as talking, but as difficult as communication."

And if you're serious about communication, especially as a married couple, then you need to come to a place where you embrace what it means to be a good listener. I mean a really good listener. Are you hearing me? I mean a really, really good listener. Good, thanks for listening!

Jack and Ellen came in to see me at the recommendation of their pastor. Things were not going very well at all. Jack had been unfaithful to his wife over several years of their marriage and Ellen had discovered these infidelities a year before they came to see me. Jack had, through his humiliation, come to a living faith in Christ and had seen his life transformed. For the first time he realized the seriousness of his actions and the hurt that they caused his wife. He was truly repentant and attempting to make better decisions as a man and as a husband. There was just one problem: Ellen was having none of it! In fact she was quite angry. All the hurt and frustrations that were stored up over a fifteen-year marriage bubbled to the surface with the regularity of a geyser at Yellowstone. And they were also, according to Ellen, quite uncontrollable. She was extremely angry and hurt, and wanted Jack to know how deeply he had hurt her.

The sessions became predictable. I would ask about the status of their marriage, and Ellen would shrug her shoulders and say, "No better than before." Jack would look at me with a look like he had just slugged down several swallows of sour milk. It was a look that said, "Do you believe how difficult this woman is?" combined with, "Can't you do something to stop her...she's hurting me!" I demurred. I felt that Ellen needed to express her anger and hurt in a safe environment so it could be heard, understood, and dealt with. Here was the second major problem: Jack was having none of it! Whenever Ellen began her recitations of the past, he became animated, angry, and lashed out back at her. "I thought this was already dealt with!" he would howl. "Why are you bringing up things that are years in the past?" he would scream.

In Jack's defense, the issues were old and they had been dealt with—sort of. During one session that I had with Roy alone, he looked at me and expressed what was most on his heart: "Make her stop! This hurts too much!" I said that I couldn't, and added that even if I could, I wouldn't. This made him angry... with me! Even though I understood his pain and anger, I told him that he was sorely lacking in one element in his role as a husband, and that was in the area of listening. He really had never actually heard his wife. He refused to listen.

* * * *

concentrate on listening

I am uncomfortable with books with lists. I'm really not exactly sure why, but maybe it's just because I am overwhelmed by all there is to do and instantly feel guilty because I'll never do it really well if I even do it at all. With that disclaimer, let me now give you a list. But let's not look at it like a list (I am trying to reframe this—typical for a therapist!), but look at it as a collection of touch points—places where you can go to evaluate and then correct your communication.

Remember we are concentrating on listening. If I could give you a gift as a couple it would be the ability to view times of communication as experiencing the privilege of hearing what actually is going on with your spouse, what he or she is thinking, feeling, hoping, struggling with, etc. It is not primarily a time where you have a chance to finally tell that insensitive husband or that demanding wife what you really think and feel. The ability to listen is one that is vital to all good communication. I am challenging you to begin to develop your listening abilities to the next level. Here are the touch points.

touch point number one: environment

There are places where I listen well, and then others where I barely listen at all. The place, frankly, where I listen best is the office where I do my counseling. First, it is conducive for me to listen. I sit in my chair, my client sits on the sofa (I sort of like that cliché) and they are a comfortable distance, not too close but not too far away. This also gives my clients a choice. On one end of the sofa they are a bit closer to me; on the other they are a bit further away. They can choose what they are comfortable with.

Second, the place is quiet. There are no distractions that will interrupt the time. The office phone does not ring, and my mobile phone is turned off (unless I forget), so there will be no interruptions. If there happens to be an interruption that's anticipated, I'll inform my client so he or she is aware of what will happen.

Third, the place is safe. Safe in three ways: first, no one will listen in. We have a sound masker in the waiting room that ensures that no listening ears will accidently hear what is being said. Second, it is safe in terms of confidentiality. The state where I live regulates all therapists and requires that in almost every case we are to keep what is said in session strictly between client and therapist. Every good therapist takes this boundary quite seriously. Third, it is safe in terms of no adverse reaction on my part as the listener. My clients often test me and will lead up to some shocking revelation with a comment like: "You're really not going to believe this." Or, "You won't think very highly of me when I tell you that..." And then when they drop the bomb (and I have to say that some of those bombs have been quite explosive) they will pause, look at me, and measure my reaction. What they want is someone to let them know that no matter what they say or have done, that they will know that they are in a safe place where they won't be instantly categorized and/or judged.

Jack and Ellen were having difficulty with finding the right environment in which to communicate. Initially, we decided that it would be my office, and that they should not try to deal with their issues on their own. Believe me they tried, but they concluded that there was really no safe place except my office, so that's what we initially decided to do, with the goal being to determine a safe place in the home, conducive for listening and relatively quiet. With two young children at home, this is not an easily solved problem.

touch point number two: time

If you were to come in with your spouse to see me for marriage therapy, I most likely would give you an exercise to do as homework. It is quite simple and probably borders on the simplistic, but I believe that couples have found it helpful in their communication process. I ask for them to set aside fifteen minutes every day to sit down and talk with each other. I also ask that each take seven and a half minutes apiece to talk, uninterrupted, while the other spouse focuses on listening to what is being said. I am almost always asked two follow-up questions when I give this assignment: "What should we talk about, and when should we do this?" My answers are: "Talk about anything you want to as long as it does not purposely hurt your spouse." When it comes to what time is best, I tell them that it is up to them. As simple as this directive might seem, in my decades as a marriage therapist, only one couple has been able to maintain this commitment for three weeks in a row. It's a lot harder than it sounds! And the main complaint is that they couldn't find the time.

How much time will it take to communicate is one of those philosophical questions that is without an answer. This is usually asked by the husband, in the same way he would ask,

"How long will it take me to recover from my knee surgery?" My rote answer is "as long as it takes," but that isn't necessarily what the husband wants to hear. Instead of arguing the exact time, let me just say that communication is a process which takes a lifetime. I've been married long enough to be able to complete my wife, Renee's, sentences, but I still have to take time to communicate. If I don't, it doesn't happen.

Years ago, Renee would make a statement to me with some regularity. She would say, "Jim Keller, we haven't talked lately." Now, I learned at an early age that whenever someone uses both your first and last name to address you, there was usually trouble a-brewin'. If my mother was the one using both my first and last name, there was usually a discovery of some egregious act that I had committed within the last twenty-four hours. If, Heaven forbid, she used "James Mark Keller" to address me, I usually started packing for foster care. So, somehow my wife caught on to that communication strategy and it works (but don't tell her that!). And even though she might be right concerning our communication, I would always protest by saying that we talk all the time. Of course that talk was of the "What are you doing today?" variety, and hardly would even get on the communication radar screen. All my protests were roundly discredited and denied the philosophical attention they deserved. Frankly, they deserved none.

Some twenty years ago, while I was in the throes of graduate school while trying to hold down a full-time job, I had an afternoon and all night to complete a twenty-page paper due for one of my classes. I got home from a business trip at noon and was going to use the rest of the day and the wee hours of the morning to get that paper off my back. Renee knew, and was sensitive to the fact that I was under this pressure. And I knew that she and the kids would be doing their own thing at least through the afternoon and into the early evening. It was the window I needed so I could have a good start on my project. I had just sat down to work when I heard our back door opening and shutting. I went upstairs from my basement office and saw my wife standing in our back hallway. I can still see her in my mind's eye, smiling beautifully at me and giving me a hug, a kiss and a welcome home. Then, in the middle of our hug, she leaned back, cocked her head to one side and said the dreaded words: "Jim Keller, we haven't talked lately." I inwardly groaned. "Honey, you know I have to get this paper done!"

Anyone who knows my wife knows she is not easily dissuaded from something she's set her mind to do. This day was no exception. My protests had the effect of love bugs in Florida hitting the front of my car on a late May day; messy but it doesn't slow the car down one bit. I paused and she said, "Let's at least do lunch." I relented and out to lunch we went. It was a good lunch, and afforded us a conversation long overdue. I, in the howling of my own busyness, hadn't taken the time to hear my wife. In fact it was so good that at the end of lunch we decided to extend the time and go for a walk to look at the fall colors. The time became magical and the communication became a banquet to two people who had been on a limited diet for far too long. The afternoon stretched into evening, we went out to dinner once the kids were cared for, and we had the best time of communication we'd had in months and maybe even a year or two. And my paper? I honestly cannot remember anything about it except that it got done, somehow, some way.

I tell you this because we are all much too busy to take the time to listen appropriately. Our schedules are packed, our crises are many, and our commitments are legion. But I want to tell you that all of us are far too busy *not* to take the time to listen to each other—time is of the essence indeed!

touch point number three: focus

As a general rule, I don't have a difficult time focusing on the really important things in life. All sports fans reading this will know exactly what I mean when I say that it's very, very important that my favorite sports team wins. And each and every one of those victories I am convinced is in some way shaped around my undivided attention. I am positive that my shouted criticisms to the television broadcasts of my favorite teams are in some mysterious manner transported to the minds of the athletes, coaches, and especially the officials so as to enable them to grasp victory from the jaws of defeat. And if they are indeed defeated, then my astute advice was once again ignored, much to their chagrin and my utter disappointment. Yes sir! My teams deserve my undivided attention.

Years ago, Renee rushed into the room where I was raptly watching the tailend of a Celtics-76ers game back when Larry Bird and Julius Erving played. I was a Celtics fan ("was" being the operative word—I'm an admitted fair-weather fan) and was anticipating a last-second shot by my team to defeat their conference rival. The urgency in Renee's voice demanded my eye contact, but not my brain engagement. As I looked at her beautiful eyes, all I heard was, "Bird has the ball, he's in the corner, he shoots, he scores!" At the conclusion of her thoughts, she asked the classic question as to whether she was heard: "OK, what did I just say?" Busted!

here are some tips i give my clients to help them focus

physical distractions...Is there anything in this room that is distracting me from being a 100 percent listener? Television, music, phones, computers, cooking meals... all of these and more can cause me not to be able to listen the way I need to.

relational distractions...Is anyone in the room or nearby that is going to take my attention away from the person to whom I'm giving my attention? Children by far are the biggest obstacles here, but they can also include extended family members, friends, and others who might be distractions.

mental distractions...Is my mind clear of my "agenda items" which could include solving some problems, carrying others' burdens, and really any concern over issues that don't directly deal with the person that I should be focused on.

emotional distractions...Am I capable of doing what I need to do as a listener in terms of the emotional energy I need to fully engage? If I am not in a good place emotionally then I probably will not be a very good listener. This point is the one I most frequently struggle with, especially after an intense day of counseling.

spiritual distractions...I have found that my ability to center in on God is directly related to my ability to hear my wife. If that area is lacking, the listening becomes much more difficult and strained.

touch point number four: body language

Being in a good marriage means much of the time doing things in a reverse (or upside down) manner. The area of proper body language is probably one of the most neglected areas. Several years ago I began speaking regularly at a local church. I spoke a minimum of three times and sometimes four each weekend. When we began doing services on Saturday, someone had the bright idea of giving me a DVD of my message so I could review it late on Saturday night and make any appropriate changes for the Sunday morning messages. I knew before I put that DVD in that it was probably a bad idea and I was not mistaken. I cannot tell you how shocked and humiliated I was to see myself speaking. I looked so…weird! I mumbled at times, had poorly timed hand gestures, at times I was too lethargic, and at times looking like I had just drunk too much coffee. And to top it all off, a Mickey Mouse/Eddie Haskell voice was spewing out of my silly looking mouth! ARRGGHH!! I don't even want to recount to you how awful and self-conscious I was the next day as I spoke. I have never to this day watched another DVD of myself speaking. It is just too—honest!

I was trained to do marriage and family therapy, and therefore trained to try to observe everything I possibly can about my clients when they speak. How they introduce themselves to you; where they sit in your office; if they're with others, how they sit in relation to them. For example, I have a couple that I counsel that could both be excellent mimes. I'm convinced of it. I never in my life have seen such clear and effective non-verbal communication! Really! The problem is that almost all of it was negative. They had all the classic defensive gestures: arms that fold across their chests, sighs that were the seedlings for hurricanes, eyes that rolled like slot machines, and finally an assortment of snorts and grunts that would make a pig proud.

Jack and Ellen were a textbook case on how body language can sabotage communication. Both were doing their best to deliver their heartfelt emotions to the other, but their body language got in the way. Ellen would purse her lips and shake her head side to side whenever Jack spoke. And Jack, upon seeing this, rolled his eyes. Finally, in an attempt to help, I began pursing my lips and shaking my head when Ellen spoke, and rolling my eyes when Jack responded. I did this for no more than two minutes when they both stopped speaking to each other and looked at me as if I had just beamed in from Mars. "Are we doing something wrong?" Ellen asked. "No, I'm just responding to each of you like you're responding to each other."

Jack was a champion that day. He not only took it, he began to feel it. His own weapon was turned back against him. He had dripped with anger and disgust, probably far more than he was aware he was projecting, and he began to soften his responses and not roll his eyes. Ellen was also a champion and burst out laughing. "Am I really that bad?" she asked. "Both of you are awful and I can't stand it anymore," was my smiling response. We went on to our most productive session, not because of a stellar therapeutic technique, but because both Jack and Ellen began to see that they needed to listen with their body language.

touch point number five: like them

When I attended graduate school I took a course on professional ethics. I don't remember the name of my instructor but she was a wise woman. At the beginning of one of our classes I remember sitting around a table and hearing her ask one of the most interesting questions I had heard in all of my grad school experience: "What do you think that clients want most from their therapists?" It certainly perked up the attention of the class as we all began to take our turn at surmising what the answer might be. I thought our answers were quite profound: "They want to know they have a competent therapist." "They want someone to sympathize with them." "They want someone to solve their problems." To each of these answers our instructor shook her head, and with a smile said, "No, that's not it." Then it was my turn and I thought I had it pegged. I said, triumphantly, "They want someone to listen to them!" But the response was again a smiling "No."

I have to admit that I was totally stumped. What could it be? We had run the gamut of every educated guess we could think of. Save, of course, the right answer. She smiled and said that what clients want most in their therapists is someone who would like them. "That's it? " I said. Her memorable response was, "That's everything." I have to admit to having been somewhat skeptical, but I am now convinced of the veracity of whatever study was done to determine that particular fact. I have seen it in decades of counseling, as I have tried to come alongside hundreds of hurting people, many of whom have done very hurtful things to others. Usually at the end of the first session I have with a client I will look at them in the eye and say, "You know, I like you." Whenever I say it, I do my best to say it with sincerity. It is quite striking to me to see the response in almost every client to whom I've uttered these words: male and female, old and young, emotionally healthy to off-the-charts unhealthy, they all soften, look at me, and respond by saying thank you.

One of our biggest challenges in marriage is to communicate

through conflict (another chapter) in a productive manner. But I will propose to you now that the key factor in making sure conflict stays on a positive path is two people determined to hold on to liking each other, regardless of what hurtful thing they have just done. Being kind wins the day.

touch point number six: compassion

The word compassion literally means "to feel along with" someone else, usually as it pertains to their personal pain and struggles. When couples come to see me I find that compassion is many times in short supply and sometimes non-existent. I don't think there are too many people who don't view themselves as capable of compassion. We tend to see ourselves in the most positive light, and the ability to feel the pain of others is something that we all know is somehow important in having successful relationships.

Years ago my wife began having severe back and neck pain. I showed the requisite sensitivity and compassion to her for at least a month. But I have to say with great regret that I soon grew tired of her pain. This is a woman that I love very much, but I found myself avoiding long conversations over her struggles, and really going out of my way to not ask questions that would lead to that subject. I'm not an insensitive man, just a selfish one—I didn't want to deal with the messiness of her pain.

Until one day while in a hurry to get to an appointment, I whipped my head around to look out the back window of my car while backing out of the garage. The sudden movement wrenched my neck and I cried out in pain. It was excruciating. I struggled with that pain through the rest of the day until I returned home to tell Renee my tale of woe. She listened with patience and empathy and suggested some actions I could take to remedy my neck. Almost as an afterthought, I took her by the shoulders and said, "I'm sorry." She didn't even ask what I was sorry for—she knew, and gently said, "Now you can understand what I'm going through a bit more. Sorry for your pain."

It's interesting to me that what we most want from others is sometimes so easy not to give in return. We all want someone to feel our pain and compassion is essential to every strong marriage.

Jack and Ellen kept going around the same block emotionally. Jack wanted Ellen's forgiveness and Ellen wanted Jack's compassion. Neither would give the other fully what they wanted. I felt that the key was in Jack's ability to understand his wife's pain and anger, not just intellectually but emotionally. Every therapist hopes for a breakthrough and usually they come as gifts given rather than planned interventions. This happened with Jack in a session with his wife. Instead of beginning with a list of his pains and grievances, he told her that he was beginning to understand the pain that he caused and wanted her to know that from that point on he was focusing on getting better so he could be a better husband for her. Instead of focusing on his own struggles, Jack chose to identify with Ellen's pain. He chose compassion. I wish I could report that Ellen fell into his arms and they lived happily ever after, but life isn't that neat and tidy. The remainder of the session was painful for Jack, as Ellen tested his new-found compassion. But that compassion over time helped him become a better listener, and the better he listened, the healthier their relationship became.

conclusion

The next chance you have for a time of communication, I would suggest that instead of saying "Let's go talk," you say instead, "Let's go have a time of listening." Anyone can talk, but it takes work to listen. And it's that work that will pay dividends as your marriage matures. So, the first upside-down way in a marriage is not to talk so much. Instead, take the time to listen intently.

[chapter 2]

quit forgiving all the time

*"Any place that does not receive you or listen
to you, as you go out from there, shake the dust
off from the soles of your feet for a testimony
against them."*

MARK 6:11 NASB

Several years ago I received a call from a woman who was
wrestling with what it means to forgive. Angie had been married
fifteen years and had three children. Both she and her husband
were committed Christians and committed to each other for
a lifetime of marriage. Divorce, as with many Christians, was
not considered an option for either spouse. But the marriage
was not a good one, and for her it had become excruciatingly
bad. Her husband Mark had emotionally withdrawn from her
for several years, pouring himself into his work and giving what
leftover energy he had to their kids. He was the consummate
successful professional: hard-working, focused, and always busy.
It was easy for him to plead overwork and fatigue, and as a
result, Angie was dying emotionally. She, though, had poured
her life into her children all the while attempting to repair and

rescue their marriage. At her initiation, they tried everything from conferences to counselors to study groups in order to find some solutions to their dysfunctional relationship. But every one of these interventions was met by indifference from the husband, and Angie was stuck in a place where forgiving Mark for his apathy would be acquiescing to his mistreatment.

She came in to see me in desperation, confused about how to have a forgiving heart and yet get through to her husband. Could I help? After two sessions I thought that I had the answer and asked her a question.

"How brave are you?"

She paused, and then responded, "Pretty brave."

"OK, then, you need to leave him."

It took a few minutes for Angie to respond. I had suggested something outside of what she had thought was acceptable. But after contemplating, and wrapping her mind around the suggestion, she responded.

"I can do that?"

"You *can* do that, and I think it's the only way Mark will understand what you're feeling." She didn't quite know what to think, but the relief in her voice was palpable; she was no longer trapped in an impossible situation.

I never counsel for a couple to get divorced. That doesn't mean that couples I counsel don't get divorced, but it is never from my direct suggestion except for the rare exception of abuse where I am concerned with the physical well-being of the wife and children (or sometimes the husband as the case may be). Also, I never counsel separation lightly. It is not usually a very good idea unless there are compelling reasons that would make becoming healthy more of a realistic possibility. I didn't think that he would understand the pain she was in through any other means. And besides, she was a strong woman, and would be able to make this decision with thoughtful conviction.

I asked her, as I do with many of my clients of faith, to pray about it and then act accordingly. As it so happened, that evening her husband asked about her counseling appointment. She shared with him my suggestion, and that she was praying about this decision. Mark was dumbfounded.

"Would you even consider this?" Mark asked.

"Yes I would, I'm praying about it," she responded.

With leaving him on the table, Mark started to see how deep his wife's pain actually was for the first time. It rocked him. But he was also highly skeptical of my counseling qualifications. Who was I to even suggest that separation be an alternative?

Mark scheduled an appointment with me the next day. He was none too happy with me, or the situation he was in. That first appointment with Mark was tense, but through it Mark began to see the condition of his marriage in a new light. Seeing the need for change, he showed humility and a willingness to learn. Mark was confused, however, that after all the conferences and Bible studies his wife still harbored the same feelings.

"But we've addressed these issues already and she's already forgiven me. Why is she bringing this up again if she's truly forgiven me?"

I explained that things hadn't improved in large part because he had taken Angie's forgiveness for granted, never repenting from the hurt that he was causing her. The light came on (like I said, he's a good man) and he admitted he needed to change his ways.

Of course God calls all of us to forgive, but that doesn't mean that we forget, nor does it mean that we don't set boundaries for the future. We would never pardon a bank robber if that robber went out and repeatedly robbed other banks. In the same way, we should not accommodate any behavior that is repeatedly hurtful and dysfunctional. Boundaries need to be formulated, expressed, with consequences made crystal clear from the outset.

As a Christian, it is not suggested that I forgive others; I am mandated by Christ Himself to forgive those who offend me. All of us are familiar with the Lord's Prayer:

> *"Our Father who is in heaven, hallowed be Your name. Your Kingdom come... Your will be done, on earth as it is in heaven. Give us this day our daily bread, and forgive us our debts, as we also have forgiven our debtors."*
>
> Matthew 6:9-12 NASB

So what does it mean to forgive? To forgive a person means that you are releasing him or her from any and all punishment for a past or present offense, no matter how badly they deserve that punishment. Any retribution that may be contemplated needs to be set aside. The offense may never be used as a weapon against the offender at a later date. So, as Christ forgave my sins, I am called to extend that forgiveness to others. This is one of the central tenets of the Christian faith.

But there is now, in our present culture, an atmosphere of what Dietrich Bonheoffer called "cheap grace." This World War II pastor, who was martyred for his faith, wrote a book that was life-changing for me: *The Cost of Discipleship*. His contention was that the assumption that God was all-forgiving was making weak and feeble Christians when it came to their living out their faith. And these feeble Christians cheapened Christ's sacrifice when they willfully and deliberately sinned, assuming that all they had to do was to ask forgiveness and all would be well. Biblically, nothing could be further from the truth. Forgiveness never releases a person from the consequences of his or her behavior.

An example of the consequences of bad behavior is found in Matthew 16:21-23. Jesus is foretelling His death when Peter takes umbrage at the words of the Savior. In fact, Peter takes it on himself to rebuke Jesus, saying, "God forbid it, Lord! This shall never happen to you (NASB)." Note Jesus' response... He did not say, "Oh Peter, there you go again. You're always so impulsive but regardless I forgive you. I guess we can't expect too much from you anyway." In case you're looking up the text, that is *not* how Jesus responded. Instead, Jesus responds, "Get behind me, Satan! You are a stumbling block to Me; for you are not setting your mind on God's interests, but man's (NASB)." Doesn't sound very forgiving, does it? Just four verses earlier in this chapter Peter is designated as the rock on whom Christ would build His church. From a rock to Satan in four quick verses! Peter is proof that even our words can get us into deep trouble and cause dire consequences.

I share all this to make this point, which I believe to be quite important when it comes to forgiveness. If we bring a sloppy view of forgiveness into our relationships, we will find it difficult to deal with and resolve conflict adequately. If I am convinced a quick "I'm sorry" will get me out of any and all consequences, then I am sorely mistaken. But the biggest cries of protest emanating from my office are those from spouses whose offenses, even though forgiven, are still causing them to reap the consequences of their behavior.

defining personal boundaries

As we begin to define boundaries, let me first give a couple of disclaimers. Healthy boundaries are put in place for our protection and for the maintenance of healthy relationships. Good boundaries keep us from being abused. Abuse is an overused word in my line of work and at the same time, in some cases, it should be used more often. Honestly, though, I have heard relatively normal behavior described as abusive and the most heinous behaviors sloughed off as the product of a "bad day." All abuse is harmful to a relationship but not all behavior is abusive. I would suggest you seek wise counsel to determine the exact status of where you are. So as we address the upside-down concept of not being so forgiving, let's talk about what healthy boundaries should look like.

boundary number one: no emotional abuse

Ben came in to see me because his wife sent him in. I always love these sessions! The men look at me like they're about ready to have a prostate exam and they anticipate they'll enjoy the session about as much. Ben was an angry guy and very tightly wound. He was the classic entrepreneur, full of ideas, hard work, and daring. At home he was distant and contentious. But as the session progressed, I found that Ben was open to hear another's perspective and that he indeed wanted to change to be more loving to his wife if he could just figure out how.

A few weeks later I met his wife Pat. She was an outgoing, attractive professional who was a good mother and was striving to be a good wife. I assured her that I would do my best to try to help her husband and see if we could bring healing to the marriage and also help him to become a better father. She was grateful and hopeful. I encouraged her to set boundaries: no engaging Ben if he became angry or hurtful with his words, and requiring that he be in counseling until significant improvement was made.

Over the next year I worked with Ben in dealing with his anger and his inability to be emotionally intimate with his wife. Ben had recently become a Christian and this was helpful in giving some clear direction in his growth. We talked about healthy ways to deal with his anger, what it meant to love unconditionally, and what his role as a husband and father should be. Ben began to not only get better, but he began to become great. I was pleased and excited for him and knew that Pat would be appreciative as well. Or so I thought...

As Ben became less emotionally abusive, Pat became more critical of his behavior. In fact, the marriage became a waiting game for Pat to identify more of Ben's mistakes. The irony was that even though she acknowledged his improvement as a husband and father, she became more dissatisfied with the marriage. Now Pat was angry and hurtful with her words. As I confronted her with this during a session, she refused to own her part in the abusive cycle. It was the last time I saw her.

The topic of emotional abuse is the most slippery of all the ones I've mentioned in this chapter. The words or actions that cause someone emotional pain usually produce a feeling that in some way, shape, or form they are being abused. I define emotional abuse as follows:

Any intentional withdrawal of affection or goodwill to cause emotional pain or any directed negative behavior to cause emotional pain is. It is also any emotional manipulation aimed to cause repeated pain.

Ben was an abuser, but the irony of his situation was that he now was being hurt in the same way that he hurt his wife. Pat had set boundaries when Ben was abusive with his words, but she refused to acknowledge her own abusive behavior.

boundary number two: no verbal abuse

When I was a kid, we regularly and with great conviction, would yell this ditty to anyone who verbally hurt us: "Sticks and stones may break my bones, but words will never hurt me!" Whoever penned those words is a liar, and when we mouthed them, we became liars too. Words can hurt a lot.

Nina was certainly someone who knew the pain that words can inflict. During her first session with me she explained that she had been married four years. It was her second marriage and she was raising two teenage boys that she had from her first. Her first husband was an abusive addict, and her second husband was different, unusually kind, attentive, loving, and a Christian. The only problem, she told me, was that her second husband was verbally abusive with her and with her boys. "How bad?" I asked. At times I've wondered whether or not angry or stressed communication can actually be labeled "verbal abuse," but in Nina's case there was no doubt. John, her husband, would have meltdowns every one to two weeks and they were emotionally and relationally destructive. His rages would be laced with the vilest profanity and he would hurl these epithets without hesitation. I asked if John was still living with her and the children and she said no. "But he's very sorry," she said. "I don't want another divorce and I love him and I know he loves me!" "And the children?" I asked. "They never want him to come home again. He's apologized over and over but still goes back to his rages. What should I do?"

For four years Nina had been forgiving and for four years she and her boys had to endure severe verbal abuse. Obviously forgiveness was not enough in moving this marriage in a healthy direction. I told Nina that he should not come home, and that she never should have him come home until he was ready to address his anger and seek healing, something which, up to this point, he had refused to do.

"How long should we stay separated if he refuses?" she asked.

"That's up to you, but if you're asking my opinion, my answer is forever."

"Are you telling me to get a divorce?"

"No, I'm telling you the boundaries that are, in my opinion, going to keep you and the boys safe from any more abuse."

Nina relayed to me later that John was not pleased with my advice. I think his response was "I thought he was a Christian counselor!" But Nina prayed about it and felt that she should set a boundary, several actually. John finally began hearing her and that hearing enabled a healing process to begin. Much has been written defining verbal abuse, but here's my definition:

Any word said in anger that is meant to cause pain in another. Any word repeated over and over in the same vein is abusive.

I am *not* saying that we should never say words that hurt. Sometimes words that hurt bring healing. When Nina told John he couldn't come home and what her boundaries for him were, John was hurt, but it was a hurt meant to bring healing, and therefore was not wrong.

But when we use words to inflict pain, and if we use profanity and call names, such speech is certainly abusive. I am frequently challenged by clients that if they just "lost it" one or two times, how is that being abusive? I asked one client how many times I would need to call him a "loser"—certainly a mild epithet by verbal abuse standards—for it to be memorable to him. "Once," was his honest reply.

Let me add that the absolute worst response that you could possibly have to a verbal abuser is to answer in kind. You will never win with this strategy, and the only thing you'll gain is abuser status yourself.

boundary number three: no physical abuse

I have lost count of the number of conversations I've had with female clients concerning episodes of physical violence. These episodes are usually described as aberrations in the relationship, and to be honest, they usually are. But they should not be dismissed too soon or forgiven too easily. And the excuses and rationalizations come out a bit too easily: "Oh, he just had a bit too much to drink." Or, "He was under so much stress at work." And then, "Well, I can be a bit annoying at times." Be those things as they may, there is no acceptable excuse for physical violence. You can never justify, let alone excuse, a man physically threatening and/or harming his wife (nor a wife harming her husband, for that matter, though that scenario is much more rare). Obviously this holds true for physical abuse of children as well.

I live in Florida, where physical abuse is defined very broadly and punished severely. If you have been physically abusive to your spouse, you will go to jail. I have to say, I rather like this system. I know it can be manipulated, like any other legal process, but I prefer being safe to being sorry.

Alex was a client of mine who was a referral from a therapist I greatly respected. She told me that he was a "good guy" but had some challenges with his temper. As we made our way through our first session, he told me about how frustrating it was to be married to his wife, and from what he described, she did indeed seem to be someone that would be a challenge to live with. And then he described his anger. Alex was a big man—bigger than me, which I always take into consideration as I do my work—and he told me of an incident where his wife accused him of physical abuse. "All I did was keep her from leaving the room. I was determined to talk it out and I didn't want her to go." "How did you accomplish that?" I asked. "I just blocked the doorway. It was no big deal." "It was to your wife," I responded. "Yeah, but you don't think I meant anything harmful by that, do you? I was just frustrated."

What I went on to tell Alex was that what he had done was considered by the state as physical abuse and that he would have been in trouble if the police had been called. I added that had his wife been the one to tell me this story, I wouldn't have let her leave my office unless she promised to make the boundary clear with him and told him the next time it happened she would call 911. He raised his eyebrows and said, "You don't think I would actually harm my wife, do you?" "Alex, I have no idea how you are when you're angry, or stressed, or maybe have had too much to drink. But I do know this," I said leaning in, "if I ever hear you've hurt your wife, *I'll* come looking for you." And then I smiled. He was bigger than me, after all. Alex was and is in his heart a good man and he heard me and embraced the boundaries necessary to never put his wife in that position again. I told him he should be thankful that he had a wife who didn't forgive too easily. He agreed.

boundary number four: no sexual abuse

I am deeply saddened by the stories of clients over the years where a father (and in rare cases a mother) systematically sexualized his relationships with his children. This abuse usually took the form of inappropriate touching and voyeurism, and in almost every circumstance the other parent knew and, due to denial, nothing was done.

One of the first families that I ever counseled dealt with a voyeur husband/father and it devastated the family, while simultaneously being swept under the rug. It was just too embarrassing to be talked about. And it was the daughter, now an adult, who bore the brunt of this emotional trauma. I cannot tell you how angry this makes me, and how sad for the now dysfunctional life of this adult daughter. Counseling is a necessary step in the healing process and needs to be sought so the boundaries remain clear and are enforced. And I must add that all appropriate legal steps need to be taken so that the perpetrator will be brought to justice.

Marital rape should never be tolerated. There is no mandate in Scripture that allows a husband to meet his sexual needs without taking into account his wife's needs and desires. Any use of Scripture to the contrary goes against what God wants us to experience in marriage. A husband is called on to sacrificially love his wife and put his needs second to hers. This would certainly apply to the sexual aspect of a marriage relationship as much as any other. I urge those women who are caught in a marriage where they are being used sexually, and not loved, to find a counselor who can help them through the process of setting boundaries and finding healing.

I must mention that pornography is a means of passive sexual abuse. I know that this is an incendiary comment and some readers might indeed even ridicule this idea, but I deal firsthand with the pain and hurt that pornography causes marriages. There's not a male alive that hasn't struggled with pornography or wouldn't struggle with it if he were exposed to it. I'm obviously a male so I'm not speaking from an ivory tower. But pornography is a killer of intimacy, and it focuses the husband away from the reality of what he needs to do as a man, namely using his sexual energy to love and romance his wife. A pornography habit that turns into an addiction is poison to a marriage.

I have counseled scores, if not hundreds of couples, where pornography had disrupted the relationship. Some time ago, a middle-aged man came into my office with a story I hear over and over. Rick was "Everyman": kind, intelligent, moral, spiritual. He loved his wife and his children. I liked him instantly. "My wife was doing some work on my computer and she happened into some sites I had been on and they were, well…" "Pornographic?" I suggested. "Yes," he winced back at me and refused to look me in the eye. I assured him that his situation was not unusual, and that he was not "sick," but I hastened to add that the consequences of his actions would have negative effects on his marriage if he didn't address them. "How do I stop?" he asked. "And will my wife ever forgive me?" Many excellent books have been written on sexual addiction and I don't have the time to go into all the details of the healing process, but this is what I told this husband and every man I talk to concerning this issue: "Stopping the action is the easy part, healing your heart is a lifelong process." (I confess to a bit of exaggeration here, but comparatively speaking it's true.)

But Rick's next question was right on target. "Do you think my wife will ever forgive me?" "Yes," I answered, "but that won't heal her pain right away, and I need you to try to stay in her pain in order for you to heal properly." I went on to explain that the actual addiction is never really the issue, it is the symptom. Sexual desire is a good thing. For a man, it's a testosterone-driven inclination toward physical intimacy. An inclination is not a perversion, but an inclination unchecked will become an addiction every time. Any addict can stop his or her behavior for a finite amount of time. Ship them off to rehab, be hypervigilant concerning their behavior for a while and they will remain clean. This is where it becomes easy to confuse the ceasing of a behavior for actual healing. It's easy to think that when the behavior stops, then the problem is over and forgiveness can be extended, to which I respond, "Not so fast!"

Yes, we need to forgive, but that forgiveness must also come with boundaries. In the area of sexual abuse, stopping the behavior is the mandatory first step, but it is not the solution to the problem. I am glad to say that Rick and his wife were able to work through not just the issue of his pornography addiction, but they were able to use that work to deal with the real issues of their marriage: unresolved anger, unspoken disappointments, lack of emotional intimacy, and poor communication. But the key motivating factor in all this was a wife who didn't forgive too easily. She allowed her husband to appropriately feel her hurt and set healthy boundaries for their relationship. And she came to understand that all addictions are heart problems and the solutions to those problems take time, really a lifetime.

boundaries that work

My client Nina's first boundary was asking her husband to leave the house for an indefinite period of time. John didn't like the boundary, but acquiesced hoping to be able to come home soon. Her second was insisting he get the therapeutic help he needed before she would ever consider having him come home. He agreed to this as well and found an excellent therapist to help him work through his anger and relationship difficulties. The third boundary was coming to see me for marriage and family work. I have to tell you, I did not like what John had done to his wife and stepchildren. His anger was extremely abusive and I wasn't particularly looking forward to the session he had scheduled with me. But I was surprised. Not only was he owning his own brokenness, the work he was doing with his personal counselor was paying dividends in how he felt about himself and how to relate more healthily to his wife and stepchildren.

He asked if I thought that he would ever be able to go home. I answered that I really didn't know, but I did say this: "If you ever rage again at your wife, you will *never* be able to go home." I didn't say it to be mean, nor was I trying to intimidate him— he was big enough to break me in half with one arm! I was just trying to be truthful. John did the best he could to take the steps toward healing himself and his marriage. There were missteps, but the bottom line was that John finally faced his issues because of a wife who decided not to forgive too quickly.

Mark and Angie continued to work through the issues that confronted them through their fifteen years of marriage. Mark began to make his wife a priority and became serious about showing her how much she meant to him. But he was quite disappointed when she didn't respond with the enthusiasm that he expected. It was very frustrating and he complained about it to me consistently. "Why is it that now that I'm really making an effort, she seems distant from me?" I responded by asking how long he had been absent emotionally from the marriage. "Nine years," he responded honestly. "Well, you have eight and a half years to go," was my response. I said this a bit tongue-in-cheek, but I was making a point nonetheless. Even though forgiveness is unconditional, the wounds of the past take longer to heal than we would like. Mark began to understand that patience was an important part of healing his relationship with his wife. Giving Angie time to recover was part of the loving sacrifice that he made to bring the marriage into a healthy place. It was my privilege to officiate in their vow renewal and to see them fully in love and committed to each other.

Not every marriage that comes to me for help turns out that way, which I have to tell you makes me very sad. I hate divorce and what it does to the spouses involved. I hate even more what it does to the children. Ben's marriage—that we discussed at the beginning of this chapter—didn't make it. Pat was not pleased with anything that he did, and I can honestly say that for years he did his best to try to find a way to make their relationship move in a positive direction. Pat, true to form, didn't just make the marriage difficult, she made Ben the enemy. He had to move forward by not being so forgiving.

The upside-down marriage is one where forgiveness is

chapter 3

stop spending so much time together

"After [Jesus] had dismissed [His disciples], he went up on a mountainside by himself to pray. Later that night he was there alone."

MATTHEW 14:23 NIV

There are two memories I have from the early years of my marriage that pop into my brain from time to time, like the bread that you forgot you were toasting until it springs up from the toaster saying, "Remember me?" I had a job in those years that put me on the road at least every other week. They were emotionally exhausting trips and took a lot of time and effort both to pull them off and to recover from them. Renee and I had two young children at home at the time and as you can imagine, being a temporary single parent was not easy on her, despite the fact she was a very capable mother.

I was convinced that when I came home from trips I was the hero, rushing in to relieve my wife from the overwhelming tasks of parenting and household chores. I imagined my arrival was anticipated for at least a day in advance, and that I brought home nothing but joy (plus, I guess, some dirty clothes as well). But two memories let me know that my vision was really a fantasy. The first happened when I had a trip unexpectedly cancelled and I had more time at home than I anticipated. "Lucky Renee and lucky kids," I said to myself. "They get to have more of me!" Renee didn't see it this way, and I learned that she felt my unexpected presence at home made me "in the way" of something she had planned to do.

I was stunned to think that maybe my physical presence at home wasn't viewed as the "blessing" that I had built it up in my mind to be. A few months later another interaction had even more impact. I had been gone on a trip for three days, but was at a location that was relatively close to our home. I asked Renee to join us for a dinner that we had planned to end our trip, and she agreed. I had missed her quite a bit and was really glad to see her and have her have the opportunity to see what we had accomplished earlier in the week. The dinner was a good one, and at an appropriate time she put her hand on mine, squeezed it gently, and moved close to whisper in my ear, "The kids and I are not looking forward to having you come home."

At first I thought she might be joking. Remember we liked to tease each other. But a quick glance confirmed that she was quite serious. Outwardly I tried to still look pleasant and affable, but inwardly I was hurt and confused. "How so?" I whispered back. She replied, "You are too uptight at home. You bark orders, micromanage the kids, and try to make sure that they're perfect. It's a lot easier to go about our lives when you're not there." I wanted to argue my point of view, but I was too stunned to speak and thought it best to rely on my favorite proverb: "Even fools are thought wise if they keep silent, and discerning if they hold their tongues" (Proverbs 17:28 NIV). It was good I held my tongue, because I needed to listen, and I am grateful that she was able to tell me something that even though she knew it would probably hurt me and make me angry, she knew I needed to hear. It made me a better husband and father to hear those words.

Now I tell you this not so much for the content of the event, as important to me as it was, but more to focus on what enabled that even to happen. Remembering that incident years later, I was struck by the fact that we probably would not have gained that clarity if we hadn't spent some time away from each other. Time away had provided a perspective that would have been more difficult to see if we hadn't had some time apart.

Of all the chapters in this book, this is the most difficult to write because this is the one that can most easily be misunderstood. Let me start with what I *am* saying. Each spouse individually needs to regularly go through the process of two things. The first is gaining perspective. We live in such a hurried and harried culture that we seldom take the time to assess where we are a couple. This takes alone time, and involves determining what do we need to stop doing, and then establishing what it is that we need to do both as individuals and as a couple. The second is what I call "looking in the mirror." Each husband and wife needs to own whatever it is that they need to own. What is it that they need to see about who they are and what they've done and not done in the marriage? This time of introspection is best done alone, and self-examination done well takes time.

But let me also add some disclaimers:

I am **not** saying that couples should live separate lives.

I am **not** saying that couples should live separately.

I am not saying that couples should refrain from spending long periods of time together.

I am not saying that couples should use separation to solve their marital problems.

A couple I saw recently turned to me at the end of a particularly contentious session and asked me who I agreed with. I said I agreed with both of them and I disagreed with both of them (vote for me!) which probably produced thoughts of, "We pay for this advice?" in both their minds. What I went on to say was this: "You both have to get away and step outside this situation long enough to stop blaming each other for the problem so you can focus on what **you** need to do to resolve this conflict. Don't spend so much time together." I explained that they needed to gain a fresh perspective, and I encouraged them to use the time for healthy and prayerful introspection, a time to look into the "mirror." I tried to stress to them that it was more important to learn what they needed to do individually, than to figure out who was right and who was wrong. But given their ambivalent reaction, I don't think they were quite satisfied with the direction in which I was taking them.

Let me spell out some of the benefits that I see in couples who are willing to afford each other individual time.

proactive time apart

I am an introvert, so I have a natural bias toward spending time alone. I am my own best company and can entertain myself quite easily. The writing of this chapter is done during a time where I'm alone for one week. So far I've been able to keep myself occupied very well. But even in the reality of my introversion I am reminded that although I like to be alone sometimes, I never like to be lonely. And as time goes by, I am more and more anticipating being back with Renee. But whenever I take some intentional time away from my wife for a week or even for an hour, I have the potential to see several benefits. Proactive time apart

gives and/or returns a sense of self. Sometimes I cannot see the forest for the trees. Actually, sometimes I can't even see the tree because my nose is jammed up against the bark! I remember Renee telling me when our children were young that she just wanted to go someplace where someone wasn't tugging on her demanding that she do something for them. "Are the kids that tough?" I naively asked. "It's not just the kids," she said, poking me in the chest. I got the message. She was losing her sense of self. I am surprised how a simple suggestion of spending time away from the family, even if only for an hour or two let alone a day or two, is met with such incredulity and even derision. "I could **never** do that!" the mother of three small children exclaimed. "How would they survive without me?" I wondered how they were surviving as she was taking time to talk to me, but I think she thought I was being a smart-aleck. "My business couldn't make it without me!" the CEO almost shouted at me. "What would happen if you got sick? How would your business run then?" "Well," he huffed, "I'm not sick." I tried as gently as I could that he really was sick…he had a sick soul.

allows for personal evaluation. A few years ago I was concerned that a friend of mine was losing his way. His marriage was suffering and he was making bad choices. I knew of a men's conference that would be an ideal environment for him to do some personal reflection. But the only way I could convince him to go was to go with him. I hesitantly agreed to go and ended up enjoying the conference immensely. My friend had a life-changing experience, but what surprised me more was that I benefited by having some time for my own self-evaluation. Ideas that had rolled around in my mind for months finally began to sort themselves out. And I was able to do a thorough spiritual inventory and it was refreshing to say the least. If Jesus had to take time away from the most important ministry in the history of the world so he could reenergize himself spiritually, then I better take the time to do it myself. So let me say here that there never will be a perfect time to get away; you'll just have to take it.

gives perspective on your marriage. When I encourage individuals to take a day or two out of their schedule, I want them to not just clear their heads but also to gain a better understanding of their marriage. Namely, what are the real issues that need to be dealt with, what areas of conflict are chronic and need to be addressed in a different manner, and what conflicts are acute and need immediate attention? Remember that this perspective is not an analysis of what your spouse needs to do, but on what your responsibility is in the marriage and then what your next right step should be. I'll never forget the client whom I encouraged getting away for a weekend to evaluate her marriage. She came back the next week and I asked her what she came back with. "A list of what my husband needs to do in order to make this marriage better," was her retort. This, I informed her, was not the goal of the weekend and was not her next right step. I don't think she ever came back after that appointment.

fuels appreciation. I have a client whose husband developed early-onset Alzheimer's. She has spent the last ten years of her life being responsible for a man that loses a bit more of himself each day. She is one of the most remarkable women I know and words cannot express how much I respect her. When we talk, there's not a session that goes by where she doesn't voice an appreciation for her husband and express sorrow that their relationship is no longer available to her. She appreciates her husband like no other person I've ever met. Time apart fuels appreciation better than anything of which I'm aware. As I type these words, I have been away from Renee for five days, and I can't wait to see her again. As the songwriter sagely says, "You don't know what you've got 'til it's gone."

remedial time apart

Let me take a bit of space here to talk about separation that comes out of painful circumstances through personal and relational misconduct. I'm often asked by clients if separation is a good thing? First of all let me say that there is no "one size fits all" when it comes to a real life situation. Your marriage is unique to you, so there is no formulaic answer to your or my problems. Second, separation has no guarantee of working. But let me add parenthetically, if your spouse comes to you and says he or she needs some time apart to evaluate the marriage, I have never seen these situations played out where the marriage stayed together, save one. And if they want you to move out, resist going as long as you can. There's no problem that two people cannot solve while they're living together, as long as they have good boundaries in the process.

The primary issues that cause separation are abuse, infidelity, and addictions. I am not saying that separation is ever a requirement in these situations, but where the pain is extremely high, or the relationship particularly volatile, then these are the issues that usually can lead to a trial separation. I personally recommend a minimum of one month and a maximum of three for these separations. This is my own conviction formed out of years of doing marital therapy. One month as a minimum allows both parties to feel the reality of the separation for a long enough time to see its reality. Any separation beyond three months tends to put couples in a routine that can be difficult to readjust if there is reconciliation. And if a separation takes place, there needs to be a plan in place that will bring the marriage back together healthier than when the separation occurs. There are three purposes for separation due to relational trauma:

beginning the healing process for the personal and relational wound.

establishing a therapeutic protocol.

working on an agreed upon reconciliation process.

Years ago a young couple came to see me with marital difficulties. Matt was a hard-driving, good-looking executive with success written all over him. He was the son of a missionary and he and his wife Susan had a strong commitment to their church. They both were also on several boards and were a prominent family in their church and community. Susan was convinced Matt was having an affair. He swore he was not. When I first started counseling I thought that I could detect when a client was lying to me. Matt disabused me of that conviction. Session after fruitless session went by with me trying to give them some positive direction and to get them unstuck. Then the call came in—Matt was caught red-handed having an affair with a family friend. It had been going on all along and it was obviously not a healthy situation. Susan wanted a divorce, Matt wanted to save the marriage and we were at an impasse. I suggested that she and Matt separate for three months. As the truth came out Susan discovered that there was more than one instance of infidelity in Matt's past, and I felt that they needed a full three months apart.

We first addressed Susan's needs. She remained in counseling and I helped her process the pain and anger that she was feeling. There were four young children involved, so we also needed to make sure that Susan had the help that she needed to run a household full of kids while Matt was away. Even though Matt wanted time with her, Susan needed some time away from the relationship so she could begin to allow her wounds to heal. She also needed to determine whether or not she wanted to stay in the marriage. This initial process was best done without Matt being present.

Matt also did one-on-one sessions where we began to examine his life so he could make some sense of his choices and then we began to take some corrective steps that would ensure that he wouldn't go down that path again. Even though he was extremely remorseful, it soon became evident to me how unhealthy he was when it came to relationships with women and especially his relationship with Susan. He did not take separation very well and wanted me to curtail the time apart and facilitate spending time with his wife. He also didn't want anyone to know of his marital difficulties and he worried that if he stayed out of his house too long it would become public knowledge. I asked him what was more important, his marriage or his reputation? He finally picked his marriage.

We then formulated a reconciliation process. We allowed for time with the children, and then after a month began to do couples therapy. In that therapy we dealt with Matt's infidelity, set up the boundaries that would need to be in place if reconciliation were to take place, and began to work on building healthy and consistent communication. Matt was eager, Susan was skeptical but open, and we began to deal with conflicts that had been unresolved for most of their marriage. The breakthrough came during a one-on-one session I had with Susan where she broke down crying saying that she knew God wanted her to forgive her husband and that the children deserved to have their father present with them if he could get healthy. I had and have great admiration for her faith and courage.

The three-month period came to a close and Matt wanted to know how the events would unfold. During a conjoint session, Susan tearfully told Matt he could come home and we began to establish what would happen after their reconciliation. It was agreed that both would continue in couple's therapy, that they would attend a marriage seminar once a year and that Matt would also continue his individual therapy. Other minor stipulations were made, agreed to and Matt was home that weekend. The reconciliation took place because they were willing not to spend time together so they could bring healing to their marriage.

Matt remained in therapy for another three months, but began to miss appointments. I called after some time, but he assured me that everything was fine and that he would be back in to see me. He never did, until three years later when he told me that he had had another affair and that he wanted to once again fix his marriage. Couldn't we go through the same separation process and get it fixed again? I told him that it wasn't quite that simple, and that it initially depended on what Susan said. When I did indeed talk to her, she told me how the last two years were filled once again with Matt's secretive behavior, and that this confirmed her suspicions. I asked her what she wanted to do, and she said she felt the only option she had was divorce. Regrettably, one year later they were no longer husband and wife. I tell you this sad conclusion because actions have sobering consequences and if there is time to be spent apart for healing and coming up with a reconciliation plan, the act of getting back together is only the beginning of the process to bring healing back to the relationship.

time apart as a healing agent

Wayne and Carol came in to see me not liking each other very much. I initially was having a difficult time figuring out why. They were pleasant, respectful of each other and seemed to have a stable home life as they raised their three children. As I began to dig a little, though, I began to see flashes of anger in Carol about Wayne and some conflicts that had gone unresolved in the past. Wayne had a temper and a tongue. But what exacerbated the whole situation was the fact that they had worked together out of their home for the last eight years. The business was successful and they both were excellent at the professional roles that they had taken on, but they were having a very difficult time making it through a day without a conflict. Here was a couple that on the outside had everything: a successful business, healthy kids, a nice home, and on top of it all, they could be together all the time. But that last point was in part tripping them up. Proximate time together is not the same as intentional time together. And if time together as a couple is not intentional, it can either keep you stuck where you are, or can even cause your relationship to suffer.

Carol didn't like Wayne any more. She didn't like the way he talked to her, talked to their children, did business, and handled stress. The first suggestion I made was to have Carol get away from the house and the business to do some personal realignment. I encouraged her to get a new perspective of herself and her relationship. The second suggestion was to Wayne: I focused him on being much more intentional in their time together, and talk over anything but the business, which was overrunning their entire lives. I suggested that Carol transition out of the business so that stress could be eliminated from her life. He began working toward that end. Wayne embraced this plan, but Carol remained skeptical. I enjoyed seeing Wayne's growth, but he was soon frustrated that he was doing all the work, all the changing, and Carol was not responding. I have seen this in dozens of marriages, where the husband begins to change and expects his wife to respond immediately. Wayne was a typical man, and an American man to boot! We want instant results—the sooner the better. I tried to give Wayne a more realistic perspective of how long this process would take. But more importantly I encouraged him to take time every day to spend intentional time with Carol, and not be satisfied with just proximate time. Will it work? The jury is still out, but Wayne is getting it and he'll never be the same. Taking time apart and using that time to regain perspective can be the healing agent that can bring new life back into a marriage.

To summarize, the mere proximity of your spouse does not guarantee that your time together will enhance and build your relationship. In fact many times it produces just the opposite effect. When couples are stuck I strongly encourage them to take some time to themselves to gain a new perspective of themselves, their spouse, and their marriage. And when the relationship is suffering through traumatic circumstances, many times taking an extended time apart becomes a necessity. Whatever your situation, be intentional with your time together, and don't hesitate to use your time alone to bring a healthier perspective to your life and marriage.

chapter 4

fight more

"Later, when Peter came to Antioch, I had a face-to-face confrontation with him because he was clearly out of line."

GALATIANS 2:11 THE MESSAGE

Rachel came in first—it's always interesting what you'll hear when the wife comes in first—and she was not happy. I have learned over the years that when wives come in first they want their perspective to be heard uninterrupted. Passionately, she explained that her marriage was all but over, and that her husband was clearly the culprit. Although she had been patient for years, her patience was being just about depleted. Based on her account of the marriage I couldn't say that I blamed her. She told me that John would nitpick, tease, and obsess over little things that displeased him. And given enough time and frustration, he would become angry and belittling with his words and then withdraw from her and the children.

After fifty straight minutes of her analysis of their marriage, I asked if he would be willing to come in to see me. She sighed and said he would. Then she added, "You know, I really feel sorry for you. You'll never be able to fix him." So a week later I had my first appointment with John. He was not what I expected. John was fit, intelligent, and a successful engineer. Instead of being angry and verbally abusive, he had difficulty communicating accurately how he felt. I had expected a sullen and angry man who had trouble stanching his anger and hostility. Instead, I found myself talking to a man who was frustrated and bewildered as to how he should respond to his wife. He too doubted whether or not his marriage could ever improve. He said, "Every time I do anything that Rachel doesn't like or she does something that I don't like, I find myself getting angry, but I know that if I say anything, she'll get mad at me. So I just say nothing until finally the day comes when I can't take it anymore and I explode."

"And your explosions are pretty bad, right?"

"Yeah," he confessed. After a brief pause I looked him squarely in the eye and said, "Well, I think I can solve your problem."

With wide-eyed skepticism he said, "How?"

"Well, you simply need to fight more."

John gave me a look that oozed with frustration, and he finally blurted out, "I am sick and tired of fighting with my wife and here you want me to do more of what has caused us problems in the first place. That makes no sense!"

When he walked out of my office ten minutes later, I doubted whether I would ever see John again. I was asking him to do the very thing that in his mind had caused emotional pain and relational discord: walk willingly into conflict.

The ironies here abounded—Rachel had labeled John as an angry person, but she was just as angry. She claimed that John was abusive with his words, and she was correct. But Rachel was also abusive with her words to John, and she often excoriated him in front of the children. And conflict was viewed by both spouses as the problem in their relationship, when nothing could have been further from the truth. *The problem in Rachael and John's marriage wasn't conflict; it was a lack of conflict resolution!*

There is a myth about marriage that is perpetuated by the experiences of a myriad of people who grew up in homes of divorce. Because marital discord is so often prevalent in relationships that end, the prevailing wisdom is that a relationship with little to no conflict is a healthy one. I realize that it is just as unhealthy to have perpetual conflict that is unresolved, but I see many marriages where both spouses have resigned themselves to a sullen silence that leads to marital isolation. People of faith also join in often with the assumption that if we really love each other as God loves us, then we will never have conflict. Nothing could be further from the truth. And couples who do not face this fact tend to run from conflict until the health of the marriage disintegrates because conflict is never resolved.

This is not to say that constant arguing and bickering is a sign of a good relationship. Spouses who bicker and carp at each other are just as stuck as those who avoid conflict like the plague. But I am continually surprised at the damage done to marriages because of conflict avoidance. It is typical to find spouses that respond to unwanted actions and words by completely cutting off communication. This cessation is often characterized by silence, avoidant behavior, and a forced conversation style that sticks to topics of normal marital functioning, like the schedule for the day and who is picking up the kids. Silence, or what marriage expert John Gottman calls "stonewalling," is one of the most devastating forms of relational punishment.

constructive conflict

Even though conflict is something that most of us instinctually wish to avoid, it plays an important part in our personal and relational growth and development. Fighting is essential for character and boundary formation. Here are some truths about conflict that I find helpful in reminding others that it's OK to fight:

conflict is biblical. When you look at Scripture through the lens of relationships, both with God and with others, there is a surprising amount of conflict that takes place. From Cain killing Abel to the battles of Revelation, there's a whole lot of conflict that is going on. And much of it is not healthy, Jesus himself went out of his way to engender controversy and really to just get people riled up. He calls people whitewashed tombs, sons of Satan, and hypocrites. He goes into the temple and whips the money-changers and tips over the tables of the merchants. The Bible by the way never condones violence, and only permits it as a last resort in desperate situations. One cannot read the Sermon on the Mount without seeing that Jesus espoused a peaceful lifestyle. He lived a life that proclaimed that violence can never be justified in relational conflict and should not be tolerated. In addition to the example of Jesus, the New Testament church is replete with conflict over who gets fed first in the church corporate meal, who gets to go on the next mission trip, and who gets to dictate the doctrine and direction of the First Century church. The founders of the Church were not conflict averse, they were conflict resolvers.

conflict is common to all relationships. This might seem to be an obvious point, but I still am surprised when my wife and I have a disagreement that grows into a conflict. And the better that we've gotten along in the days before the conflict, the more surprised I am when it happens. But being in a marriage is a constant reminder that two people mean that there will be two different views on issues, two opinions as to what to do next, and many times two wills pushing in those two different directions. From where we should eat to where we should live, two differing opinions can lead to an impasse and a conflict, even after three and a half decades of marriage. As a therapist I often hear people complain that they just want to be like the "_____" (you can fill the blank in with the name of your most ideal married couple). The "Andersons" (as we'll call them) are the couple that is always smiling, always cordial, always (appropriately) affectionate, always getting along. They never fight! I used to try to refute such observations logically, but that has never seemed to work so well. So now my tongue-in-cheek response is, "Oh, the Andersons? The Andersons have been in therapy for ten years and their marriage is a mess!" Of course I'm using therapeutic deception, but it's worth it to see the initial look on my clients' faces. I then tell them that I was counseling the Andersons last week and they told me that they wanted to have a marriage just like theirs. By now I let them know I'm teasing, but I want it to be an effective delivery package for the truth—the outside of the package is many times quite inadequate in truly understanding the condition of a marriage. Conflict is common to all marriages.

conflict is inevitable. My favorite type of couples counseling is pre-marital counseling. The reason for this is that it's so refreshing to have two people come into my office who actually like each other! They are so happy— but one of my goals in doing pre-marital work is that they understand that conflict is going to come to their relationship. Usually this comment is met with looks of incredulity and shock. I remember one young woman, squeezing her fiancé's hand, who said to me, "Oh, we never have had a fight and we never will, right honey?" And with that she snuggled into the loving arms of her admiring but ignorant future husband. It's cute, but I have to resist the urge to lovingly shake some sense into them. I have the unenviable responsibility to bring them into reality. "Oh, it's coming," I responded, "and when it does, it's not going to be very much fun." The look on her face was only matched by the look of sorrow she had the next session I met with them. "Well, you were right," she said. "It came and it was awful."

Joe and Bonnie were the clearest example to me of the inability to anticipate conflict. They met over the Internet, and their profiles matched perfectly. They were ideally suited in every way, at least that's what the computer said. Both had been married before, and both had raised their children virtually by themselves. Joe was the president of a humanitarian organization and Bonnie was a professional in the medical field.

As they told me their story, I was caught up in their excitement in finding each other and in their joy in being in each other's presence. Since they lived in separate states separated by hundreds of miles, they wanted to get married as soon as possible so they could enjoy being with each other and so their children could start their new schools at the beginning of the school year. I was certainly open to that direction except for one disconcerting fact: they had only begun talking three months ago! It was a tough next three sessions, as I tried in vain to slow them down. But they were not to be denied. As two older, successful, and mature individuals, they felt like they knew what was best. Pastors, friends, co-workers, and mentors were all consulted and universal in their responses: slow down a bit. I have to confess to being more on the optimistic side of these issues; I hoped that they could pull it off if they continued to get good counseling.

Two months later they were married. Twelve months after that, they were divorced. And while it might not seem surprising to the casual observer, I was both surprised and dismayed. When the marriage began to disintegrate shortly after the wedding, Joe called me to let me know that the marriage was not going well.

"Joe, what happened? What went wrong?" I asked.

His response was short and to the point: "Jim, you were right. I think the main problem was that we forgot to fight before we married."

Now I don't encourage couples to fight for the sake

of fighting, but I do want them to experience conflict and to see each other in conflict before they make a lifetime commitment to each other. Joe and Bonnie began to argue almost immediately after their wedding, and it went downhill from that point on. They saw each other in a different light that was more difficult to overcome than they had anticipated. Bonnie's anger was something that Joe had never seen, and the fact that Joe tended to shut down his emotions in conflict was certainly not what Bonnie had anticipated. What began with great joy ended in great sorrow because two very mature people forgot that conflict was inevitable.

conflict is an opportunity. Dave and Karolyn were in trouble. They came to counseling angry with each other and unable to have a fight that produced anything but rancor and distance between them. Both were extremely intelligent, extremely successful, and extremely juvenile when it came to fighting. Dave was the classic "the best defense is a good offense" fighter, and Karolyn was his perfect foil, the sniper who waited for the right shot, and that shot was usually lethal. This pattern had gone on for years and they were in a desperate place. And, I was informed by Dave in no uncertain terms that I was the last in a long list of therapists and I would probably be no more successful than the others. After their first session I informed them that I would like them to do some homework and they said they would be willing to try anything. I then told them that I would like them to fight more than what they were doing. Dave didn't hold back: "Are you nuts?" he exclaimed. His wife told him to be more respectful to me and he told her to mind her own business and I said, "Now that's what I'm talking about! Just like that!"

Dave reluctantly agreed to another session and when they returned the following week, I asked how it was going. If body language was any indication, it wasn't going very well at all. Dave was red in the face, and Karolyn was slumped in her seat, unable to make eye contact with me. "It is worse than ever," exclaimed Dave. And, when I asked if they did their homework, Karolyn glumly nodded her assent.

"So what did you learn?" I asked. "What did you want your conflict to accomplish?"

Both sat sullenly there waiting for the other to answer.

Finally Dave said, "I learned that my wife will never see things as they really are, and that our marriage is irrevocably broken."

"I disagree," I responded. I took a Socratic approach, introducing a series of questions: "What do you understand about your spouse that you didn't before? What do you understand about yourself that you didn't before? Did this conflict cause growth, both spiritually and relationally? Did this conflict increase your ability to function well as a couple? Did this conflict enable you to face issues that you haven't faced before?"

"I can't think about all those things when I'm in a conflict," Dave huffed. "It just isn't possible!"

Dave is a hard-working and brilliant professional, successful in business because he is willing to work hard and care for his clients. But here he was telling me that he just couldn't pull off something that would improve not only his marriage but his whole quality of life. So I told him, "I'll buy that you haven't thought of these issues this succinctly before, but I will never buy that you cannot discipline yourself to think through these things when you're in a conflict."

Karolyn then joined in and said, "He never thinks of me during a conflict, just himself and he is extremely hurtful with his words." Thinking that she was off the hook she leaned back with a look of satisfaction: her husband had been called out! "What about you, though?" I asked. "What are your responses to those questions?" "It's not my conflict," she said. "I don't want to fight; I just want to get along." I told her as kindly as I could that I didn't believe her. "I think you don't like the fighting, but I don't think that you just want to get along. You're responding with verbal jabs and sucker punches that are just as hurtful to Dave as his words are to you. So, if you're going to fight, and you are, you better do it intentionally and with a purpose behind it." Now all three of us were experiencing healthy conflict!

Here are the touch points, then, for using a conflict for positive ends:

use each conflict to gain understanding of your spouse, even if it's something that you don't particularly care for or about. Understanding is essential in any conflict resolution.

use each conflict to gain insight into yourself. The shortest path to growth is one that is laid out by someone who loves us enough to be honest with us.

use each conflict to grow up a little more. Maturity is the goal for all who are serious about reaching their potential, and successful conflict resolution is one of the accelerators to personal growth.

use each conflict to increase your working together as a team. Conflicts expose strengths as well as weaknesses. Wise couples can accomplish together far more than they could individually.

use each conflict to expose unaddressed issues you have personally. This will help you continue to be a student of yourself, which is critical in your growth and maturity.

Dave and Karolyn began to digest these points and I then gave them some tips as to how to have a successful fight. But all the conflict resolution techniques they could possibly learn would be ineffective if they didn't know what the purpose of fighting actually was. Once they owned the positive goals for conflict, they were ready for the how-to's.

how to fight fair

Eight principles for conflict resolution:

I have to first say that it's a lot easier to write dispassionately about these principles than put them into practice during a conflict. But over time, if you have both spouses committed to a healthy resolution process, these steps will become invaluable in saving you time and keeping you on task.

1. equal time: Every couple is unique, but usually one spouse tends to be more verbal and the other less verbal. This of course gives the debate advantage to the spouse who has less difficulty expressing himself or herself. Because of this, I impose time limits on how long a spouse can speak uninterrupted. That limit should be no more than three minutes. And equal time needs to be extended to both spouses. It's very tedious to stop to time a spontaneous conversation, but if it's agreed to ahead of time it can be very helpful, especially to the spouse who is less expressive.

2. no absolutes: As a marriage therapist, I have spent countless hours listening to couples engage in conflict. The "no absolutes" boundary, by far, is the most violated boundary in this list. In the heat of the battle, absolute language is used to drive home the point and to let the recipient of such language know the depth of the pain his or her dysfunction has caused. Statements such as, "You always…" or "You never…" are used regularly, and can put the receiving party totally on the defensive, which is at the time probably the desired effect, but in the long run leads to frustration and no resolution whatsoever. If you use absolutes, you might well win the battle, but you'll end up losing the war. The use of absolutes is usually an assault on someone's character, and not a correction for their behavior. Character assassination is a sure-fire way to ensure that the conflict will not be resolved. I elaborate on this a bit more in Principle #6.

3. opinion v. fact: Observations and opinions must be stated as such. Own your own opinions and state them as such. Instead of saying, "You had an awful attitude when you came back from that trip," or, "You had way too much to drink at that dinner party," it is imperative that you use language of personal ownership. "It seemed to me that you had an awful attitude when you came back." or "I am of the opinion that you had way too much to drink." Stating opinion allows the one communicating to say in no uncertain terms how she or he feels, but allows for difference of opinion. This is a crucial principle so that the conversation doesn't get stuck in the rhetorical ditch and the real issue can surface and be resolved.

4. only two people at a time: Conflict that involves more than two people is almost impossible to resolve. Stick to the topic at hand with the people at hand. The additional person/people may or may not be physically present, but if they are brought into the conflict in any manner, the chances for resolution are practically zero. When I hear a spouse say, "And I'm not the only one who feels that way." I know I have a long and difficult session ahead of me. I will quickly attempt to head off that conversation by saying that we need to stick to the people in the room and the opinions of just those two. Minding this principle will have the added benefit of not putting the children in the middle of the conflict, which causes a legion of issues down the road. When children are triangulated into marital disagreements, they are always put in an impossible situation, which leads to frustration and anger on their part. Keep them out if it!

5. only one issue at a time: I usually explain to my unexpecting new clients that because they have a male therapist we will only be able to solve one problem at a time. The response is usually one of "Is this guy kidding or what?" but I assure them that I am not. If you find yourself in the middle of a conflict and start saying, "But what about the time you…" you have violated this principle and have complicated the resolution process by a factor of five. You are always on a slippery slope if you begin to compare your faults to the faults of your spouse. Own what you need to own and stop the comparison game.

6. issues not character: Statements that impugn a person's character are not going to readily lead to conflict resolution. "You are a liar" versus "I think you are lying to me" are worlds apart in their implication and impact. One is an indictment on the person's character; the other is a step toward solving a specific conflict. Now, the person to whom you're talking may indeed have a bad habit of lying, but calling them a liar makes for poor conflict resolution. The only way couples grow together is by owning their issues choice by choice. It's only then that they can begin to own the larger issues of their own character, and do so in a more positive and nurturing environment.

7. win/win not win/lose: This boundary is for all you competitors out there who hate to lose (people just like me!). I don't mind admitting I'm wrong as long as I feel that I can also make my point and get some of my complaints heard. This is an approach to resolution destined to fail. If I am serious about learning what I need to learn, then I will only focus on the part I play in conflict resolution. Trying to play God with my spouse is destined to not only fail, but to frustrate as well. Win/win scenarios only come about when each spouse focuses on his or her own issues. If at the end of a conflict both parties can say they heard what was being communicated to them, they felt heard by their spouse, and they came to own their own issues, then a win/win scenario has just taken place.

8. time limits: I can potentially save you hours of frustration and a deepening of whatever issues you're dealing with if you would just hold to this principle: keep your conflict time to a fifteen-minute limit. If at the end of those fifteen minutes either of you feels stuck and/or frustrated, then suspend communication for at least an hour and no more than twenty-four hours. If you are making progress, go on for as long as both of you think the conversation is positive and effective. If just one of you wants to stop temporarily, then that needs to be respected, as long as the issue is not ignored for more than 24 hours. I cannot tell you the couples who go on for hours with the same conflict making no headway whatsoever. Talk about frustration! Make sure you mind the boundary of time limits. If you both can mutually agree to time limits, I am of the opinion that it will help you get to the point of the issue and not get caught up in peripheral issues.

Dave and Karolyn had no initial success at all. In fact, I had to admit with both their evaluations that things were getting progressively worse. Dave was getting angrier by the day, and Karolyn was more depressed and passive-aggressive in her response to his meltdowns. I would role-model for them what good communication looked like and where it could ultimately head. Two sessions later, Karolyn arrived at the session on time and Dave called in to say he'd be ten minutes late. Not expecting a positive response, I asked her how it was going. To my surprise, she said that Dave had an "attitude change." Instead of being angry, he began to show her kindness through a listening ear and a more positive outlook on their marriage and problems. I had an individual session with Dave one week prior to this appointment, and Karolyn looked at me with wide eyes and asked, "What did you do to him?"

This is the time as a therapist where you would love to share some great intervention or clever technique that basically turned the tide. All I said to Dave the week before was that I wanted him to talk to her as if she were his best friend with the goal of enhancing the friendship after every conflict. As he began to do this, Dave had begun to think through why in fact he was angry, what he wanted the conflict to produce, and more importantly what he wanted the conflict to produce in him. Meanwhile, I'm still trying to figure out what I did right.

chapter 5

have less sex

*"Flee from sexual immorality. All other sins
a person commit are outside the body, but
whoever sins sexually, sins against their own
body. Do you not know that your bodies are
temples of the Holy Spirit, who is in you, whom
you have received from God? You are not your
own; you were bought at a price. Therefore
honor God with your bodies."*

I CORINTHIANS 6:18-20 NIV

It was late Friday night, and I received an emergency call from a man who needed to see me right away. Calls like these are familiar in my profession, and as I usually do, I quickly assessed how serious the issue was. Doug, while not at risk to harm himself or others, insisted that he come in the "sooner the better." Early the next week we scheduled a time to meet. When Doug came into my office he looked like he hadn't slept for days—he was bedraggled, with dark circles around his tearful eyes. The first, woeful words out of his mouth were uttered in desperation: "She won't have sex with me anymore!"

Sexual dysfunction is a painful and frustrating predicament to be in, but it is not what I would consider to be an acute crisis situation. Somewhat baffled and frustrated, I sought clarification as to the extent of his predicament. I've worked with couples who haven't had sex for years, so I realized that he could be really hurting. "So how long have you been on your sexual fast?" I asked.

He lowered his head into his hands, softly weeping, and muttered, "One week...seven whole days."

I struggled to feel empathic toward Doug at this point. I had been married at least ten years longer and a week without sexual intimacy was for me more analogous to going without dessert rather than a forty-day fast.

"A week doesn't seem that long," I suggested.

"You don't understand," Doug continued, "Jill and I have had sex every day since our wedding day, except when our two children were born. It's what we committed to and now the whole foundation of our marriage has been shaken."

After two hours processing Doug "crisis," I thought it would be a good idea to have his wife, Jill, come in for a marriage therapy session. Even though I hadn't met her, I had a good idea where she was coming from in this marital stand-off.

"Can you help me?" Doug pleaded at the end of that first session.

"I think I can, but you'll have to commit to weekly sessions and it will help if I can meet with Jill too."

"I can do that and I think she'll come in to see you too. But what can I do in the meantime to fix this? What should I tell my wife?"

"This is what you say to your wife: 'I am going to spend some time trying to understand where you are emotionally in this marriage, so I will respect your "no-sex" boundary until you think we're in a place where it can be lifted.'"

"What if I don't see it quite that way," Doug said, with more than a trace of whine in his voice.

"If you want to work with me, that's what you have to say and eventually that's what you'll have to own."

"But will I ever have sex with her again?" he asked.

"I'm not sure…" was my dangling response. Facing his own existential dread, at that point Doug knew it was best not to ask any more questions.

*   *   *   *

We live in a sexually charged society. Our culture is inundated with sex, sexuality, and sexual innuendo. This sexualization across all domains of our culture has presented unique challenges to marriages trying to thrive today. Sexual mores have changed, sexual expectations have intensified, and varied sexual experiences are more common. So what should be a couple's attitude toward sex, qualitatively, and quantitatively, coming into marriage? How does a married couple successfully navigate the treacherous waters of our sexualized culture?

Doug had done it by the book, at least by the book in terms of what many Christians believe. He came into his marriage a virgin, which he saw as a feat of Herculean proportions in our day and age. He did it because he believed that God meant sex for marriage: namely, a committed lifelong relational covenant where two people together explore the height and depth of emotional and relational intimacy. Along with Doug's many healthy convictions and his mature approach to marriage came one that was not so healthy. Now that sex was "legal," Doug saw sex as a right, not a privilege. In his words, he would spend his married life, "making up for lost time."

Doug's view of physical intimacy became a type of relational leprosy that attacked their marriage by numbing emotions. He made physical sex an idol. It wasn't that Jill didn't enjoy sex or physical intimacy, it's just that after years of numbers-driven sex, she began to feel that she was no longer a participant but an object to be used for Doug's personal pleasure. Doug had deluded himself into thinking that Jill was an equal in their physical relationship, but over time she became increasingly angry and withdrawn, culminating in becoming totally shut-down emotionally and relationally.

Men and women view sexual intimacy in distinctly different, but complementary ways. For men, sex equals emotional intimacy. It's not that a man cannot feel close to his wife without sex, but the culmination of that intimacy is physical and sexual. For a woman, sex is more the icing on the cake of marital intimacy, but not the cake itself. Frequency tends to be more of an issue for men than for women, but interestingly enough, in my experience the clients who complain most vociferously about a lack of physical intimacy are my female clients. The whole concept of frequency is influenced strongly by what motivates each gender to be physically intimate. Men have more testosterone than women, and that fact gives them what is termed a "sex drive." They are the initiators, the ones who generally take the lead in sexual intimacy. Women, on the other hand, do not have a "sex drive." They certainly have sexual desire, and a longing for physical intimacy, but they are in no way compelled biologically in the same way men are toward physical intimacy.

Our culture, of course, has turned all these differences upside down and inside out. A woman now is encouraged to be more the aggressor sexually, and she is "rewarded" for her performance by continuous attention from men, and if she continues to perform well, perhaps even the security of a long-term relationship. And I suppose this would be more acceptable if sex were merely a function of our biology, our "drives," and had no greater significance than that, save for a few fleeting emotional benefits. But I believe sex is more than that, not just because I am a Christian, but because of the countless hours I've spent talking to couples about their sexual relationships. Their desire, both male and female, is for something more, something transcendent. And the Apostle Paul addresses this transcendence in a most unusual manner in his first letter to the Church at Corinth.

The Church of Corinth was a rather unruly band of believers dealing with all sorts of issues, many of which were sexual. For instance, there was a man living with his stepmother in an openly sexual relationship. Others in the church were availing themselves of the city tradition of "worshipping" at the temple by visiting the temple prostitutes. The modern-day equivalent to this would be the pornography industry. The utilitarian view is, "Hey, our sexual desire is natural so why not everyone benefit from it. No harm, no foul!" But Paul says there is a foul and it does cause harm. Why? Because the theme of marriage all through Scripture, from Genesis to the epistles of the New Testament is that two people become "one flesh." So Paul is arguing that even though you might think that sex is "casual" or utilitarian, there really is no such thing because sex involves not just physical connection, but emotional, relational, and most importantly, spiritual intimacy.

For marriages such as Doug and Jill's where sex has been reduced to emotionally detached physical intimacy, healing requires a slow rebuilding of holistic intimacy. While there is not a one size-fits-all formula to healing, here are six principles to building true physical intimacy:

1. **focus on quality not quantity**: Sex is one of the most talked about subjects in our culture but one of the least understood in terms of its impact on a relationship. Having the spotlight so much on frequency and technique are killers of marital intimacy. Quality is so much more desirable than quantity and it can be achieved.

2. **focus on your spouse**: I am continually surprised by statements that men make concerning focusing on the needs of their spouse. I hear statements like, "I think I'm an excellent lover because I take care of my wife's 'needs' first." Understand that a man desires to have an orgasm with each sexual encounter he has, that's the norm, but making his desire the desire of his wife is nothing short of narcissism. I am not saying that women don't desire orgasm, but it usually is not the *summum bonum* that it is for a man.

3. **discipline your desires**: When talking to men about their sexual desires, the topic of discipline always comes up. Many times I will ask couples to temporarily suspend sexual activity in their marriage so they can focus on emotional intimacy. I do this because sex

can provide a false sense of security in a marriage, functionally being an avoidant mechanism, and not dealing with root issues. The response I hear most from men is, "Give up sex—that's absurd. If I can't have sex I'll explode!" A couple of years ago I was doing a session with a couple and during this time I suggested that they suspend sex for a brief period of time. The husband gave the old familiar refrain, but instead of trying to argue him out of his position, I looked at his wife and asked, "Do you have any video equipment at home?" The question surprised her a bit, but she responded, "Yes we do." I then said to the husband, "Would you please inform your wife as to when the explosion is about to happen. I've never seen one and would like to have it recorded." As I recall the session, the husband wasn't too pleased with the direction this was going, but his wife simply leaned back in her chair and smiled.

News flash! Men don't explode if they don't have sex! Discipline gets a bad rap in our culture, but it's the only way to live healthily. All our desires need to come under some kind of discipline if we want our lives to be full and meaningful. Discipline isn't just stopping an activity; it's prioritizing one activity over another. So I asked Doug to discipline his natural desire for sex with his wife, and put that energy into communication that would bring healing to their relationship. It took work, and discipline was involved, but it was work that paid great dividends. I also eventually asked Jill to discipline herself not just to go through the motions of "having sex," but to do the work of communicating her desires to Doug, and to not use their sexual relationship as a means for punishing him for past wrongs.

4. keep your priorities straight: The goal of physical intimacy is not mutual orgasms. The physical pleasure of sex is merely the enjoyable by-product of something far more substantive: relational intimacy. Relational intimacy transcends physical nakedness. It is psychological, emotional, and spiritual nakedness where two individuals become one holistically. When emotional intimacy suffers, physical intimacy will eventually suffer. As Doug entered this reality, he also entered into a world of new possibilities. What he took for intimacy was really just a dim reflection of what it could be. The real work involved in having a vital physical relationship with your spouse is not work done by reading sex manuals and visiting sex therapists (helpful though they might be). The real work is done by communicating your heart to your spouse, appropriately exposing your weaknesses and struggles, and loving your spouse unconditionally as he or she works through the problems and dysfunctions that we all face as human beings. And the work that Jill was called to was now to focus on how to help and support her husband reorder his priorities, and not hold his past faults against him.

5. be intentional about your intimacy: This point, interestingly enough, is one that causes all kinds of pushback from married couples. "What! You want us to plan intimacy? That's a contradiction in terms." On and on the argument goes until I ask, "OK, then what's your plan?" One couple I counseled begrudgingly agreed to plan some time in their busy schedules. When I asked if they wanted more input the wife said, "No, you've already taken the mystery out of our lovemaking." I actually felt a bit guilty when she said that! When they returned for the next session, I asked how the homework went, and they both said simultaneously, "Awful!" and they gave me a look that said, "And we know whose fault it is." I said, "Let me guess, the time you allotted for your intimacy was in thirty minute segments, right?" They looked at me as if I were a psychic. "Who told you?" they asked. I went on to tell them that no one had to tell me because that's what most married couples think about when assigning a time to their intimacy. As they were preparing to leave at the end of that session, I asked them to set aside four hours for their next intentional time. Now they looked at me as if I were a pervert! "You want us to have sex for four hours?" the wife shrieked. "No, I want you to become more intimate in those four hours. Talk, touch, relax together, laugh together, and somewhere in that time frame, enjoy each other physically. That's what I want you to do." They came in for the next session beginning to have a deeper understanding of what intimacy is and what it could be.

6. monogamy: perhaps this is an obvious point but monogamy is essential if one is to experience deep emotional intimacy with his or her spouse. I am often surprised that spouses believe they can find true

intimacy with someone other than their spouse. True intimacy is not attained when you have online affairs, are a regular partaker of the pornographic images that are easily available at the touch of a button, or are presently in an extramarital relationship where your emotional energy is being focused. There is no way around this: monogamy is essential to intimacy.

Doug began to put his focus on the right goal: intimacy. In order to do this, he had a lot of work to do on himself. Of particular focus in therapy was Doug's relational development, and especially how he learned to relate with others in his family-of-origin. He had to deal with past sexual attitudes and experiences, and what he felt about what defined his own sexuality. He had to deal with his view of himself, what it meant to lead and love as a man when he had no model from which to learn. Jill had some issues to deal with as well: she had a painful sexual past which involved sexual abuse and promiscuity. She also had to confront and deal with a mental health condition called dysthymia, a pervasive low-grade depression that she had dealt with the last two decades. There were no quick-fix solutions. Doug, however, rose to the challenge. He began to embrace the "less sex, more intimacy" model, first intellectually, then emotionally, then spiritually. As a result, he began to grow in areas of his life that had been dormant and decaying. He came alive and with that new energy he focused more than ever on what it was to lead and love. Over time Jill responded, but it took longer than Doug could have ever dreamed initially. Even though it took a long time, if you asked him today how to have a good and vibrant sex life, he would smile and say, "Have less sex, but have more intimacy!"

chapter 6

be worse parents

*"Children, obey your parents in the Lord, for this
is right. 'Honor your father and mother"—which
is the first commandment with a promise—
"...that it may go well with you and that you may
enjoy long life on the earth."*

EPHESIANS 6:1-3 NIV

There was no question about it: the situation was serious. Greg, a seventeen year old junior in high school was found by his mother passed out on his bed after overdosing on his father's pain medication. He was rushed to the hospital, stabilized, and then admitted to the psychiatric unit for observation. After two days of psychological assessment and prescribed medications, Greg was released with the recommendation that he receive counseling to help deal with his emotional and relational health.

When I met with Greg, he seemed like a normal, emotionally engaged young man who had simply been going through some academic and relational difficulties. We talked through the struggles he was dealing with at present and came up with a treatment plan that I felt would address these issues and hopefully make him more resilient to deal with any problems that might arise. It was a good first session and my prognosis was that Greg simply needed some space to talk about some of his internal stress and develop some new coping strategies. Then I met with the parents...

Greg's mother and father were appropriately concerned following the revelation that Greg had been abusing drugs, particularly after his overdose. The more I talked to them, however, the more I became concerned for the parents. They weren't just worried about Greg's emotional health; they were worried about his GPA, his sports performance, his "questionable" relationships, his Christian testimony, his reputation, and his ability to be accepted to the college of his choice. And secretly worried, I think they were worried about how their reputation as parents would be sullied if word got out that Greg had a "drug problem". While these concerns were legitimate, they didn't get to the real heart of the issue.

During the next session, I asked Greg about his parents' marriage. His described it as "fine," but when asked to elaborate he revealed some important dynamics. "Are you closer to your mother or father?" I asked. Without hesitation he answered he was closer to his mother.

"Who aggravates you more?" I followed up.

"She does."

"Do you feel close to your father?"

"No, not really," he said.

Greg also talked about his general experience at home. "I feel as if I'm under a microscope and that if I don't perform up to expectations, the whole family will fall apart."

"Are they good parents?" I asked.

I'll never forget his answer: "They're too good! I feel as if it all hinges on me—how the family is doing, what the mood is at the house, and whether we're going to have a good time or not."

In Greg's family, the husband and wife were too devoted to their parenting and not focused enough on their own relationship. Greg's parents had every right to be concerned. No parent wants their child to suffer and to become emotionally stuck to the point of self-medication. They were right to bring Greg to counseling to see what could be done. But the key issue besides stabilizing Greg's behavior had nothing to do directly with him. It had to do with his parents. Our culture is kid-centric. It is hyper-focused on raising great kids. Not average kids, not "C" students, but above-average, excelling children who will somehow validate the family and make every parental sacrifice worthwhile.

The problem with this focus, however, is the fact that many times marriages and the relationships between the parents themselves are put on the back burner in the name of being more effective and loving parents. This is usually not a conscious decision, but one that takes place over years of family growth and child development. When a child is born into a family, the focus is of necessity on the care and protection of this new life. Wonderment sets in and the parents rejoice in every new developmental event. Interestingly enough this is a time of great stress on the marital couple. Sleep deprivation, a lessening of attention given to each other, lack of physical intimacy, and the realization of the hard work of being a caretaker to a little being who is totally dependent on its parents—all of these factors work against marital intimacy and can threaten the health of the marriage.

As the children get older and mature, there are other roles they can play that can work against the marriage. Again, these roles are almost always subconscious, but they are assumed because of both real and imagined benefits to both the parent and the child. And these benefits many times are realized at the expense of the marriage relationship. These assumed roles fall into four main categories:

1. children as affirmers: When marriages suffer, children can easily get swept up in the drama of the conflict. When I first began counseling I worked with a couple who dealt with communication challenges and an inability to resolve conflict. As counseling progressed, the wife gained more ability to voice her concerns and she began to tell her husband that he was manipulative bordering on abuse whenever he voiced his disagreement with his wife's opinions. The husband, while claiming that his wife was exaggerating, admitted that he could improve his communication style. But even though we worked at him speaking with more compassion and empathy, issues arose that kept the couple in nearly constant conflict. As the couple separated for a period of time, their son, who was an only child eight years old, was caught up in the middle of the drama. The son, Andrew, was used as a "witness" to validate both spouses' points of view.

"Andrew is very frightened of his father," his Mom told me on several occasions. "Whenever his father comes home he runs and hides and doesn't want to interact." "Andrew claims that I am never mean to him and that I don't scare him," declared the father. "When we're together, we have a great time bonding father to son. He always says that he wants to continue our times together." Because I was just beginning my counseling career, I assumed that one of the spouses was not being truthful. But over time the truth revealed itself: Andrew was communicating those things to each parent individually, and even though they were contradictory, they were accurate reflections of what Andrew actually was saying *and feeling* at the time.

Children are unwittingly used many times as pawns in the back-and-forth of marital conflict. And just as often, sensing their new-found importance to the family, children will insert themselves as the arbiter of the marriage, many times to their own personal advantage. I eventually communicated to this couple that even though Andrew was of great importance in the family and needed to be shown love and attention, he was the secondary issue in their family, the first being the healing of their marriage. "The best thing you can do for your son," I told the couple, "is to love each other well, and work out these differences." Making a child the judge of which parent is right, or healthier, or culpable, is to put that child in an untenable and emotionally harmful position.

2. **children as redeemers:** I have a confession to make: I lived my life vicariously through my son during his adolescence and early adulthood. There, I feel better already! Actually I don't think I was totally self-centered in making my son such a central part of

my life, but there were certainly some self-focused if not selfish motivations on my part. I wanted my son to have advantages and opportunities that I didn't have. I wanted him to succeed where I failed and I wanted him to become what I had failed to become. He played the sport I played (soccer, the beautiful game) and he was a more accomplished player than I was; he played the instrument I wanted to play (the trombone—my arms weren't long enough); he went to the college that I wanted to attend but couldn't (my parents couldn't afford it); he went into the profession that I currently work in (mental health counseling), and he's working on his doctorate degree whereas I only have a master's degrees. I suppose there is nothing too dysfunctional about all this, but in looking more objectively at my role as a parent, it's become more clear to me as I grow older that I subconsciously desired that my son serve an important role in my life: I wanted a redeemer.

It is normal as a parent to want your children to do well and in essence have an improved life over the lives we led as children and adolescents. In fact, this is one of the joys of being a parent. When this focus becomes too intense, the success or failures of our children reflect not only on us as parents, but as people in general. In families of strong faith, there can be a tendency to have even higher expectations of children because of the calling to a higher moral standard. The tendency then, in spite of all the parental denials, becomes wanting their children to be better than everyone else, which is couched in loaded terms such as, "I just want you to do your best" or "Just live up to your potential." This then becomes a heavy burden for the child, but could I suggest here that more to the point of this book, it also becomes a heavy burden for the marriage? Instead of each spouse looking to the other for encouragement and emotional support, children become the "redeemers" that will fill in the emotional void created by a struggling marriage.

In Greg's case, his mom and dad had struggled in their marriage for years in spite of appearing healthy from the outside. Greg's mother began to look to him for emotional support at a very early age because of her disappointment with her husband. She was bound and determined to raise children that wouldn't be disappointing. So what appeared to be good and devoted parenting devolved into extreme psychological pressure on Greg to be and provide what his father could not. Greg inevitably buckled under the pressure of unrealistic and unhealthy expectations.

3. **children as surrogates**: Every marriage and family therapist worth his or her salt knows the term "parentified child." It has a broad meaning but the consequences of such a designation tend to be serious if not dire. Parentified children are emotional and relational spousal substitutes, filling in for an emotionally and/or physically absent parent. One of the overwhelming realizations of my profession is how many children and adults have a history of being parentified children. Years ago I was in session with a sixteen-year-old boy whose mother asked me to see

him because of his difficulty in handling stress. He was chronically ill, had insomnia, and couldn't seem to gain weight. When I met him, I liked him immediately. He was warm, sincere, and eager to please. He was one of those adolescents that adults, upon meeting and spending time with him, talk to their friends and spouses in hushed tones with statements like, "Do you believe this kid? What did they do to make him so nice—so responsible?"

The problem in this family wasn't this young man's performance. His performance was as close to perfect as I've ever seen. He was a straight-A student, president of his class, the presumptive favorite for the yearly character award at his Christian school, and volunteered his time on weekends to spend time with young boys who had no father at home. So the problem wasn't one of performance, it was one of position. His father was in and out of the house, an admitted but unrepentant alcoholic. His mother and his younger brother were emotionally dependent on him, especially since Mom had designated him as "the man of the family." Plus the fact that Mom used him as a sounding board for her emotional distress, and in the name of processing, he assumed the role of husband. I have to say here that none of this was done selfishly and certainly not maliciously. Mom needed help, younger brother needed help, and sometimes even Dad needed help, and the older son felt that he was up to the challenge.

I encouraged the mother to make sure that she not

process the marriage with her son, but she told me that no one else understood like he did and no one loved her like he did as well. And you know, she was right—but the concern I had was that the price being paid for this support was too high. Her son was coming to a point of emotional and physical breakdown, and she couldn't see it. I encouraged her to focus on her marriage and to begin to process, in counseling if necessary, with her husband. She listened but failed to follow through.

At the end of my one and only session with this young man, I leaned forward on my chair and said, "You know, you don't have to take this burden on. In fact, the reason that you're not sleeping and dealing with your physical problems is probably because you've taken on too much responsibility for your family, especially your mother. Why don't you let me take care of your mother and father as best I can and let you concentrate on being a teenager." He smiled and without hesitation responded by saying, "No, that's OK. My Mom needs me and no one else will help her like I can." "But don't you want your father to be the one to do that?" "I don't think my mother believes that that will ever happen," he said. There's not one thing in that entire session that he said to me that wasn't true: he was indeed the best and most loving resource his mother had. The problem was that not enough chance was given to move the marriage toward healing, and it had a devastating effect on the family in the long run. Six or seven years later I learned that the young man had taken his own life and that it had been a shock to everyone in his family.

He had seemed so normal and totally responsible. It was a stark reminder to me of the emotional and psychological danger that can be present when a child becomes a surrogate spouse.

4. children as distractors: We all have had the experience of having the proverbial "black sheep" in either our nuclear family or certainly our extended family. The uncle that relatives whisper about during family reunions or the teenage daughter that has fallen off the radar with rumors of scandal. There are myriad theories as to why certain children act out in a certain manner, and these theories are focused mostly on problem children. It's certainly not unusual to have children go against the family norms and mores when there is discord between the parents. But many times this acting out seems to come out of the blue, with no discernible cause and little in the way of effective solutions.

I thoroughly enjoy my adolescent clients, partly because they're so honest, and partly because they're not mine. The clients in this category that are most enjoyable are the ones who are willing to work toward figuring out a more effective way of making their individualistic statements. Lori was fifteen and a self-described "wild child." Her behavior was full of rebellious acts such as drinking, curfew breaking, and sexual promiscuity. Initially, she didn't have the first clue as to why she acted in this manner, but later on in therapy we began to realize that the real conflict was with her mother, and that her mother was continually under stress due to a rocky relationship with Lori's father. Lori's mother took her stress out on her daughter, and in turn, Lori paid her back in spades. The focus of this family revolved around Lori as the "identified patient" and I can tell you that she enjoyed every bit of the attention!

As I began to work with Lori's parents, we began to focus more on the marriage and less on Lori's acting out. Both her parents loved her dearly, but that love had become overwhelmingly controlling and dysfunctional. I encouraged them both to lessen the goal of "fixing" their daughter and focus more on fixing their relationship. It certainly was never Lori's intent to cause her parents' marriage to become rocky, but her emotional response to the turmoil in the family was one that took the attention off the marital dyad and onto fixing her. I encouraged her parents to not be so devoted to fixing their daughter and to allow her to work through her issues in counseling and with trusted youth workers in her church. The main focus then became the healing of the marriage, which had the long-term result of providing a healthier environment for Lori to finally stabilize and show less destructive behavior.

Here are five principles that can help balance working on your marriage while attempting to raise children:

principle #1: the marriage comes first

spousal love covers a multitude of parental sins.

Many of my clients, both adult and children, have experienced tremendous anguish because of marital conflict in their past or present home. One of my most distressing times as a therapist was working with a nine-year-old first-born child, who was experiencing debilitating headaches that consumed his life. In tears he would tell me of the emotional pain that his parents' fighting would cause him; he couldn't escape the anguish that the conflict between his parents created him. The only thing I knew to do for him at that time was to cry with him. When I tried to intervene in this boy's parents' marriage, his mother and father told me that the subject was moot because the marriage was ending in divorce. Needless to say the headaches continued.

It is certainly appropriate for parents to raise up their children in a manner that will enable them to function as healthy and mature adults. Parenting, however, is a learn-as-you-go process, and each child requires different parenting skills. It certainly is easy to be distracted with this process, and many times the marriage relationship suffers as a result.

principle #2: parenting is a team effort

Salvador Minuchin, one of the founding fathers of family therapy, based his whole approach on the maxim, "Parents must be in charge of their children." Minuchin's wisdom, while at first glance might appear simplistic, offers profound insight into the structure of the family. Children know instinctively how to divide and conquer. And if there is disagreement as to how a child should be directed or disciplined, the family is set up for potential chaos and the marriage is weakened. Marital discord creates a chaos where children will be in charge. A divided marriage not only brings discord to the home, but many times the husband and wife will seek to curry the favor of their children instead of their spouse, validating their feelings through their children rather than their spouse.

This principle is violated with such frequency that I sometimes shake my head in amazement. A few years ago I counseled a couple that was working through some extremely difficult issues. They had two pre-adolescent children and were at loggerheads over what type of parenting style was appropriate. The wife claimed her husband was a severe and unreasonable disciplinarian; the husband claimed his wife spoiled the children to a "ridiculous degree." This intense disagreement occurred more often than not in the presence of one or both of their children, and their parenting styles became a more deeply entrenched unresolved conflict. As the marriage disintegrated, the husband shied away from his draconian parenting style and began relating with his boys in a way that he had never done—he spent one-on-one time with them, and began to listen more closely to not just what they were doing but how they were doing. Instead of the wife being pleased, she became more and more agitated, convinced her husband was turning the children against her. I attempted in vain to try to have them talk through their parenting strategies, and then as a couple come to each child when parenting decisions needed to be made or the child needed to be disciplined. The conclusion is obvious, if the marriage is suffering, parenting will also suffer or at best be extremely challenging.

principle #3: quit entertaining your children

We live in a media-dominated culture. I carry a device that I can slip into my pocket that though Internet access, phone calls, television programming, text messaging, and email, connects me with the entire world. I wouldn't have dreamed this was possible just five years ago. It is now a world of constant information and perpetual stimulation. I have seen this unprecedented access to information translate to a frenetic parenting style that pushes children to excel in sporting activities, music, dance, and other assorted amusements and distractions our culture offers. I was recently talking to a young couple about their family schedule. In addition to their church activities which required participation at least two days of the week, their children were involved in team sports and related sport camps, dance lessons, and drama classes. While all of these activities are in and of themselves worthwhile, the number of them and the intensity of the instruction were almost incomprehensible. "What would happen if you took a year's sabbatical and just worked on being a family?" I asked. The parents were speechless at this suggestion for a brief period of time, and then the wife finally responded by saying, "But what would we do with them?"

What would they do indeed! How about spending time together as a family, having a family dinner every evening and after homework and other household chores talking or participating in family games? Family nights have been in vogue for a while, but they tend to be absent-minded add-ons that promote physical proximity rather than genuine interaction. Watching a movie together as a family is fun and reasonable, but that activity is not a substitute for times where there is interaction and discussion. When was the last time you read a book out loud as a family? Or when did you last discuss some current issue as a family and seek to hear each person's opinion?

How do your children see you interact with your spouse during those times? So stop entertaining and start communicating!

principle #4: let your children make mistakes

A couple came to see me to deal with a variety of issues both marital and familial, but their central focus causing the most consternation was their teenage daughter's interest in a boy who was in their eyes less than stellar. Kristi was a bright, pretty sixteen-year-old girl who they saw as the perfect daughter. Her interest in a boy had a jarring effect on her folks. "This boy has tattoos and piercings!" exclaimed her mother. "And he runs with a bad crowd," the father added. They went on to tell me that Kristi had dated this boy for about three months before they finally stepped in. They told her she could not date this boy any longer because she was making a "serious mistake." They explained the negative direction her relationship could take and the bad influence of her boyfriend. Kristi feigned agreement, but secretly kept seeing her boyfriend until her disobedience was discovered. Kristi was told in no uncertain terms she must stop and she nodded her head. But still the relationship continued and once again she was found out. This continued back and forth for another two months and there then ensued what I call the "take-away game." Kristi's privileges were stripped one by one, until she basically went to school, came home, had dinner, and went to her room. Her computer was gone, her phone was confiscated, and she was isolated from any item that would cause her the smallest bit of pleasure in her home.

"How's this working out for you?" I asked with a smile. The smile was not returned. I tried a different approach, "How is this affecting your marriage?" This question caught them a bit off guard, but they both admitted that their relationship was strained at best. Their daughter was a huge distraction and they had found themselves bickering about what direction to go and what disciplinary steps to take next. The time and energy that they were concentrating on their daughter was seriously interfering with their marriage. They asked me what direction they should take.

"First, give her everything back," I said. I pictured that Kristi by now was sleeping on an air mattress in her totally stripped-down bedroom with nothing on the walls but lists of chores and reminders of agreements she had made with her parents. She might as well have been in juvenile detention. "Won't that validate her behavior?" the mother asked. "No, it will just let her know that you recognize that what you're doing is not effective and that you are rescinding the punishment. "Then," I said, "sit her down, express your desires, and review the boundaries that you have set for her. After that, pause, look her in the eye, and say, 'We have taught and hopefully modeled for you what good decision making looks like. But we cannot control your life and we cannot keep you from making what we think are serious mistakes. So we'll continue to set family boundaries which we expect you to honor, but we will not micro-manage your life any longer.'" The mother looked in in horror as I suggested this. "Do you know the bad decisions she could make?" "I do, and I hope she doesn't. But the price that you're paying as a couple and as a family is too great. You cannot let your daughter dictate the environment of your family."

Kristi didn't get better right away, and she did make some mistakes, but she no longer controlled the family by her behavior.

I am certainly not encouraging negligent parenting and I'm also not saying that parents shouldn't intervene when their children are making life-threatening decisions, but mistakes are potentially life's instructors—we all learn the hard way! Kristi's parents' marriage was strengthened, and that produced a healing effect not only in their relationship but in their family as well.

principle #5: let your children reap their own consequences

One of Jesus' most fascinating parables is the story of the prodigal son. That one story is so loaded with lessons that you could spend a decade studying it and still not plumb its depths. The younger son comes to the father and asks for an early retirement. "Give me my inheritance!" he cries. The father, instead of refusing, acquiesces and allows his son to not only to become wealthy but also to leave the family. As we know, the son goes off, squanders his inheritance, and returns home destitute and humbled. One of the great lessons of this story is the fact that the father allowed his son to reap the consequences of his own decisions. He did not intervene or bail his son out of trouble or out of debt. He only prayed, awaiting his son's return.

Of all the responsibilities that come with parenting, I believe allowing children to reap their own consequences is by far the most difficult. Any loving parent doesn't want his or her child to suffer the results of poor decision making. I am regularly asked to counsel adolescents who are described by the parents as "under-achievers," which I've finally determined is a fancy word for lazy. "John just isn't getting the grades he's capable of," said one mother who recently came into my office. John was in a prep school and was pulling in B's and C's. As I talked with John it was evident that he himself knew he wasn't performing up to the level to which he was capable. "What's the deal with school?" I asked. "Oh, I just don't care that much and don't want to do all the work they want me to do to get A's. B's and C's are OK." I talked with the mother at the end of the session and told her that I thought John was a fine young man and that he was doing well. "But what about his grades?" his mother asked, "He won't be able to get in to the colleges that he wants to with grades like that." "Have you told him this?" I responded, but I confess that I already knew the answer. "From the time he was in middle school—he knows what he needs to do." "Then let him reap what he has sown," I said.

John knew that his behavior had consequences, but hadn't quite reaped them yet. But behavior doesn't dictate character, character dictates behavior. John was in the process of having his character developed. His parents needed to allow that to transpire, even if his path was not totally to their liking. John got into a middle-tier college and went on to do quite well in his early adulthood. I had a conversation with him five years later and he said to me, "You know, I know I could have gone to a better college if I had worked harder in high school. I realize what my parents were trying to get me to understand." "Could they have done anything different to change your behavior?" I asked. "No, I just had to learn for myself," was his sage reply.

conclusion

Parenting is a great responsibility and a great joy, but it can also be a great distractor. Our lives are so inextricably linked with our children that it sometimes can be overwhelming emotionally. My most emotional moments and the majority of my tears were engendered by my kids. But my children eventually left home—can you imagine?! And my wife and I were the ones that remained. And the really interesting thing to me is that our relationship is still the backbone of our now extended family. Don't focus so much on your parenting that you forget that the most important relationship in your family is your marriage to your spouse.

[chapter 7]

embrace poverty

*Do not store up for yourselves treasures on
earth, where moths and rust destroy and where
thieves break in and steal. But store up for
yourselves treasures in heaven, where moths
and rust do not destroy, and where thieves do
not break in and steal. For where your treasure is,
there your heart will be also.*

MATTHEW 6:19-21 NIV

John and Brenda were bubble babies. That is, their lives
represented the confluence of the right profession, hard work,
a strong economy, and the housing bubble of the early 2000s.
They were young (barely into their thirties, attractive, and living
the good life. I found it difficult not to envy them with their 1-4
million-dollar house and their continuous success in business.
Their primary issue was common to many marriages, namely,
how John would balance his work and personal life. Because
of the myriad of opportunities with which John was presented,
he found himself working later and later, while Brenda was
at home caring for their two children less than three years of

age. Neither spouse had grown up in a wealthy family, and the money John was able to earn was new and exciting to both of them. But this new-found wealth came at a high emotional and relational cost. Conflict increased in direct proportion to the hours that John worked.

"All you think about is money!" Brenda exclaimed during a marital counseling session. "That's not true!" John countered. "I am thinking primarily of you and the kids and trying to make sure that you are all well provided for." The conflict would rage back and forth with Brenda claiming that she didn't care how much money they made and that she didn't care if they lived in a hut as long as John was home more for her and the kids. I attempted to help them structure their schedule to try to accommodate both needs. We worked on scheduling in date nights and family nights, with Brenda giving a bit on an occasional evening where John needed to work. But in the long run their problem was not one of scheduling their time; it was one of coming together in their attitude toward money.

After seeing them on and off for two years, Brenda and John came in for an appointment that I'll never forget. Both of their faces were serious and sober and John informed me that they had received some troubling news. One of John's partners had left the state and had cleaned out hundreds of thousands of dollars from their joint business account. I asked what this meant for their financial status and Brenda said, "We're broke." Their lives were literally turned upside down. In conjunction with sudden loss of liquid assets, the economy began to slow down to the point of going into a recession, and John's profession was devastated. An income in the high six figures was now reduced to just barely making a profit. They spent the next year moving from their house into an apartment, selling their expensive cars for inexpensive used ones, and began living from paycheck to paycheck. And as these challenges continued to mount, their marriage was put to the test even more. John was depressed about his professional status and inability to climb out of the hole they were in, and Brenda had to adjust to living in an apartment with literally one-fifth of the space they had in their house. Their struggle went from making necessary marital adjustments due to excess, to one of survival due to scarcity.

John and Brenda's story is the story of millions of couples that have experienced the "Great Recession" of 2008-2009. And that recession continues at the writing of this book. Couples have dealt with financial challenges not encountered on this large of a scale since the 1930s. I always marveled at my parents' frugality when I was growing up in their home. They were never cheap, but they were careful, and always lived below their means. My generation of baby boomers changed all that, accelerating spending and reaching for "better lifestyles" that continued through the beginning of the new century. But the collapse of housing and the subsequent slowing of the economy has left couples struggling to live in a solvent way as never before seen in my lifetime. Studies have continually shown that money is the number one reason that couples argue, and I find this is true with many of the couples I counsel. When the marital conversation changes from the topics of budget and lifestyle to that of mere survival, the impact is of biblical proportions. So, no matter what financial issue you're dealing with as a couple, we first need to dispel some myths before we work on some fundamental principles when it comes to money.

myth #1: money makes you happy

While this is something we all claim to know, we live otherwise. My most miserable clients are my wealthiest clients, hands down. Bill and Lynn were clients, with the recurring issue of finances—how much was being provided, how it was handled, and proper limits with children. Bill felt that he was being used by his wife and children as simply a provider of funds for their personal happiness and fulfillment. Bill grew up in poverty, and his financial success was a proof to him that he was someone with substance and a person to be reckoned with—it gave him a positive sense of self. But he lived in constant fear that one day his wealth would vanish, and with it, his self-worth. "Money doesn't make you happy, Bill," I said to him during one session. "Tell me something I don't know already," he growled back in return. "I am convinced that having too much money is a curse and not a blessing. Everyone assumes it will always be there and I feel constantly taken advantage of."

Years later, Bill and Lynn returned practically penniless, their business having collapsed with the economy. They came to see me to discuss a parenting issue but I was amazed to find them so positive. "We've lost almost all we made," said Bill with a wry grin, "but I don't think we've ever been happier." He went on to explain that their lack of funds made their lives immanently more simple, and they were able to focus on the important parts of their marriage, and weren't distracted any longer with managing their wealth. Not everyone is as positive and as adaptable as Bill and Lynn. But if you really believed money could not make you happy, why do you still work so hard? Why is it so difficult to turn down the next wealth-generating opportunity?

myth #2: money brings security

Notwithstanding the fact that it is advisable to have a cash reserve, there is no way that money can make anyone secure. All the fail-safe financial schemes promoted in the '80s and "90s of the last century have been universally debunked. If you are a saver, good for you, and if you're able to save as a couple, it's all to your credit. But security does not come from your on-hand cash; it comes from knowing that you are consistently and unconditionally loved.

Inga was the wife of a wealthy executive who had worked his way from a management position to president of a multi-national corporation. They as a couple had more money than they could have possibly imagined at the beginning of their marriage. Mark, Inga's husband, informed her one day that he felt that their marriage was stale and would be benefited by his moving out so that they could "fall in love again". Inga was devastated. She immediately suggested counseling and Mark reluctantly agreed to attend a joint session. He remained unmoved, however, by her entreaties to stay in the marriage. "Look at all we've accomplished," she pled. "What a waste for us to not be in a place where we can enjoy it together." Mark claimed in anger that he didn't feel they had a connection any longer and refused to work on the marriage. Later on, as I was talking to Inga alone, she said, "I thought that with all we had I was the most secure wife in the world. What more could I ever want? But what I didn't know is that my husband had left me two years ago emotionally." Mark, a victim of his own success, began a relationship with a woman younger than his daughter, a woman that found his wealth quite attractive. The marriage ended in divorce, a painful reminder of the futility of money's capacity to buy happiness.

myth #3: money makes you free

I doubt if anyone who reads this book has not had a time when they've played the "What would I do if I won the lottery?" game. Admit it; you've dreamed about this at least once in your life. There is a freedom that is immediately felt by not being constrained by what something costs. But that freedom is a false freedom, an illusion that portrays the myth that wealth will set you free. My experience has taught me instead that wealth can be a prison.

Art came to see me because he and his wife had fought about his work for years. Over time, Art advanced in his company to a point that he was one of the top three executives in a Fortune 500 company. He would spend a week on the road, come back to his company's headquarters in a city where it was impractical for his family to live, and stay there for another week to work out of the company office. He was only able to see his wife and three children every other weekend, and you can imagine what a whirlwind visit that was twice a month! Mindy, Art's wife, said that she was getting used to him being away, and the she and the children had a routine that they'd established that was livable. I asked if she enjoyed the set up and she said that she missed him greatly, but couldn't coax him out of his lifestyle. I asked Art why he lived in this way, and he said, "I just have a few more years with this company and when I cash in my stock options, I can retire early." It was then I realized I was up against the American dream: early retirement!

The irony, of course, is that there was zero freedom in Art's financial portfolio, as substantial as it was. He was paying a price to work like an indentured servant for another five to seven years in order to cash it all in. I told him emphatically that the price, the relationship with his family, was too high. He eventually moved home to his family and took a lesser position in his company in order to prioritize his wife and children. They lived comfortably financially, but were much happier relationally.

myth #4: money brings respect

All men want to be respected. This is as close to a universal truth as I can come up with. And on the heels of that truth I would say that all husbands want to be respected for the work they do to bring financial provision to their families. "I'm doing this work for you and the kids," is the mantra of many overworked husbands, who desperately want their hard work not just to be understood but respected. I have bad news for those husbands: your hard work is appreciated, but the money you make not only won't buy you love, it won't even garner you respect. Bob, a consummate entrepreneur, was caught up in the delusion that his hard work would bring respect from Pat, his wife. He made several successful six-figure business deals early on in his marriage, but instead of Pat respecting her husband's business acumen, she began to fear how he was handling of his new-found wealth. As Bob stumbled in his investment decisions, he began to feel the pressure created by his financial losses both at his job but more acutely at home. Pat began to second-guess his business decisions and to become agitated about the money that he seemed to lose as quickly as he gained.

As Bob and Pat continued therapy, they began to realize that what Pat actually wanted was Bob's involvement with their children and time spent with her. As he began to realize that respect revolved more around his connectedness and not his portfolio, he began to make conscious decisions to increase his time and involvement at home. Interestingly enough, Pat's respect grew.

The primary principle that connects all these myths is one that is seldom embraced in western culture: couples who deliberately choose to live with less will strengthen their marriages. In other words, taking deliberate steps toward a moderate lifestyle is a key element in dealing with the financial conflict in marriage. Embracing poverty is not a capitulation to hopelessness but a mutual determination that the marriage relationship will not be controlled by the abundance or lack of money. Couples that are not focused primarily on "getting ahead" and making sure that they will have ever-increasing wealth are couples that have taken a large step toward focusing on what will in fact allow their marriage to grow and flourish.

There are several suggestions I give to couples that I believe will help focus them on toward an appropriate and helpful mindset toward money:

step 1: agree on a budget

The concept of budgeting is for most couples a "no-brainer." No one who is serious about dealing with finances can go long without budgeting their money. But I am continually surprised at the number of couples that do not have a carefully thought-out budget. It is typical in marriage to have one spouse who is the "spender" and another who is the "saver," but even the spouses who have a more conservative approach to handling money many times have difficulty formulating a budget. A couple I have counseled on and off for years has stumbled in this area repeatedly. They don't struggle with having the money to spend; they struggle with how to manage their spending. Carl and Lisa have continued over the years to make attempts at budgeting, and Carl, who is the more conservative of the two, can come up with an impressive looking spreadsheet. But when it came to implementation, Carl couldn't seem to be consistent in his own implementation of the plan. So the dance looked like this: Lisa would ask Carl if she could buy some furniture, and Carl would agree but not give a fixed dollar amount. Lisa would go out, buy the furniture, and spend too much money, according to Carl. But because the dollar amount wasn't fixed going into the purchase, Lisa would complain that Carl was doing a bait and switch. These are two intelligent, college-educated people who cannot do something that would be basic to the most casual observer. Why is budgeting so difficult to do? I think there are two primary reasons.

First, budgeting is restrictive. It takes discipline to keep a budget, and a disciplined lifestyle is a disciplined lifestyle. So if $200 is set aside every month for household purchases and an opportunity to purchase a much-desired piece of furniture occurs, the tendency is to reward ourselves immediately, even if the piece of furniture costs $500. As we say in my family, "We can't afford not to buy it!" People don't like to be restricted, and this attitude permeates the vast majority of marriages in our country.

Second, budgeting causes conflict. I guarantee it! When funds are limited, and they usually are, then there is a finite amount of goods and services that those funds can purchase. So will it be the new dress or the new mower? Will it be the football tickets or the dinner out? This is the stuff that conflicts are made of. And generally speaking, no couple heads willingly into conflict. So, instead of taking the logical and healthy step of making a budget, couples avoid it because they don't care to go into a more disciplined lifestyle and they don't want to do battle with their spouse.

Carl and Lisa finally followed a budget and it was initially painful for both of them. Carl hated conflict and Lisa hated the type of discipline that their budget required. But they persevered and were able to come to a place where the handling of money was no longer going to be the elephant in the room. They grew in their discipline, their communication, and their ability to resolve conflict.

step 2: save 10%

I am not nor will I ever be a financial planner. But I do know some basics about money that were taught to me by my parents. My father and mother loved to save money. I remember growing up feeling that they were a little obsessed with it. Their goal was to always have a buffer, and they seemed never to be living on the edge. They embodied the profile for the classic saver: you always set something aside before you spend. I don't know if they were always able to do 10%, but I do know that they never seemed to be thrown off by unexpected expenses.

I cannot tell you the number of couples who have absolutely no savings whatsoever. Nothing... I suppose that the difficult economic times have driven more and more people dipping into or completely depleting their savings, but it is amazing to me that saving seems to be such a foreign concept, even to the wealthy. I remember a couple who informed me that they were going to have to declare bankruptcy. They ran their own construction business and had done exceptionally well for fifteen-plus years. When I asked if they'd put anything aside to protect themselves from situations like they were now in, the husband said, "I rolled everything I earned back into the business. I didn't think I ever would need to set aside cash. I thought my business was my savings account." The only savings that counts is putting cash aside. I would advise not to neglect it.

step 3: give 10%+

If ever there were a list of touchy subjects, charitable giving is probably close to the top. Everyone likes the concept of giving, but the actual practice can many times be another matter altogether. Charitable giving is viewed by many as something to be done when we have an excess of funds. After all, aren't the most famous contributors the wealthiest? Bill Gates and other multi-millionaires are considered the ones who should be able to give out of their excess. I remember being struck two years ago when reading a book on managing money by a frequent guest on the Oprah Winfrey show. He devoted a whole chapter to the topic of giving and said that even though he didn't understand the exact reason why, almost all of the wealthy people whose money he managed and many others that he knew of gave away a significant portion of their wealth on a regular basis. I have found this to be true with the couples I counsel as well.

Sam and Diane were long-time clients of mine that had dealt with a myriad of issues regarding their children and extended family. They were quite wealthy, and after years of very hard work and wise investment they were looking to slow down and enjoy an early retirement. Then tragedy hit them seemingly out of nowhere. A trusted business partner had disappeared and stolen millions of dollars of business funds. Not only were Sam and Diane hit hard, so was a long list of investors that Sam had relationships with. Sam's partner went missing for months, and when he surfaced, he informed the authorities after his arrest that he had squandered the millions he stole and that the money no longer existed. Sam could do nothing but work harder and try to begin to recoup all the funds that were lost. He refused to declare bankruptcy and instead promised to make good on all his debts.

During this devastating time, I distinctly remember a conversation I had with Diane and Sam, in which we were talking about the stress of dealing with a loss of this magnitude. Instead of despair, they both expressed a sense of purpose and even gratitude for the blessings that were in their lives and the opportunities that Sam had to see the situation rectified. "And, the great thing is," Sam said, "that we haven't cut back a dime on our giving." I knew Diane and Sam well enough to know that they gave hundreds of thousands of dollars to their church and other mission organizations. I was incredulous! "Even with your losses?" I exclaimed. "We know that the only way to work through this is not make money our god. Giving gives us the reminder we need so we won't lose sight of this." I watched as Sam and Diane recovered from their financial devastation and I'm convinced that their willingness to give to others even in the face of their own personal need, enabled them to healthily navigate their own financial turmoil without having it negatively affect their marriage relationship.

step 4: don't spend money you don't have

When the topic of money comes up with couples that I counsel, I'm often reminded of the Charles Dickens novel *David Copperfield* and his endearing character Wilkens Macawber. In and out of debtor's prison throughout the whole of the story, he gives young Copperfield the best advice his experience can offer: "Annual income twenty pounds, annual expenditure nineteen pounds, nineteen and six, result happiness. Annual income twenty pounds, annual expenditure twenty pounds ought and six, result misery." You don't have to be knowledgeable in English monetary nomenclature to get the message: spend more than you make and you'll end up very unhappy indeed.

Why is it that this warning goes unheeded in the majority of households in our country? My guess is that it's a logical consequence of the overwhelming desire for immediate gratification. We want what we want and we want it NOW! I remember one couple I counseled who had over $30,000 in credit card debt. I encouraged them to confront this issue, see and financial specialist, take a Dave Ramsey course, and go to a cash only system. After an excellent beginning, I remember talking to the couple three months into their three year journey to become debt free. "How's it going?" I asked. "Not so great," said the husband. "I don't think we can do this," the wife joined in. When I required as to why, the wife shrugged her shoulders and said, "It's just too hard to wait." "Wait for what?" I responded. "The stuff we want," was her immediate answer. I watched helplessly as this young couple once again strapped the burden of debt onto their relational backs. It was depressing…

The problem with debt is that it imprisons, and the initial enjoyment of having "stuff" gives way to the reality that material things cannot come close to making you happy, let alone a marriage successful. Couples that have determined not to do life on credit give themselves a leg up on setting their priorities straight and keeping their marriages safe from the stress of always owing the creditor.

step 5: live on a limited income

As I write these words, the income of an average

married couple is lower, relatively speaking, than it's been in over eighty years. The incredible economic boom of the last two and a half decades has stalled and stopped dead in its tracks. Jobs that were easy to come by and afforded job seekers a choice are no longer available. I heard recently that out of every job offered there are twenty people waiting to fill that position.

One of the most important questions you can ask regarding personal finances is how much money is enough. And this is just as important if not more important for a married couple to determine. This is more than what kind of a house you want to live in or what kind of a car you want to drive, even though these are an important part of your determination. These decisions get to the heart of what you want your life to be all about.

Jim and Kathy came to see me for some family of origin and in-law issues they were dealing with, but we were soon discussing their marriage and its strengths and weaknesses. During these discussions their finances came up. Both had attended prestigious colleges and had received excellent educations. Their degrees were highly marketable and they were well-connected in their community. Jim held down a very high-level executive job and Kathy worked until they had their first child.

What impressed me about Jim and Kathy was the fact that they chose to live on a limited income. They both felt that they didn't want their lifestyle to drive them to make poor decisions concerning their marriage and family time. They had purchased some property on a lake with the intention of building their dream home on the land. As they got close to their planned date to begin construction, Jim came home one evening and said to Kathy that he had some hesitations about beginning the project. He felt that the economy was unpredictable and didn't know if building a new home would be wise. Kathy mentioned that they were in danger of violating their limited income boundary, and Jim crunched the numbers and found out that she was correct. On the basis of their initial commitment to not spend beyond a certain level, Jim and Kathy decided to sell the land and stay in the home they were presently living in. I commended them for their wisdom, and one year later they saw the prudence of their decision when housing prices fell an additional 25%.

So how much money is enough? I would suggest that you would do well to determine to live on less to ascertain what you really need. It will add strength to your marriage and allow you to focus on the issues that are truly important.

step 6: don't work so much

Earlier in this book I mentioned clients who worked way beyond forty hours per week. Coming from a German background, I was raised admiring people who worked above and beyond what others expected.

My father's favorite saying was "If there's work to be done, you better be the one working." This depression-era advice permeated my psyche by the time I was a young adult. When I suggest that you don't work so much, I am not saying that you shouldn't work hard. Hard work, well done, brings joy. But spouses that work too many hours have difficulty dealing with their own stress, and then difficulty in handling anything challenging in their marriage or family.

As I shared earlier in this book, and learned this truth the hard way, with my physical and emotional health greatly compromised due to overwork. But the battle for balance continues to this day. I constantly have to limit myself when it comes to my working hours. It would perhaps be appropriate to comment here that men tend to get their affirmation from profession, while women get theirs from their relationships, primarily their marriage and family. Therefore, the conflict over working hours can be tilted in one direction or the other, depending on the whether it's the husband or the wife. And the reality of diminishing finances can work against the couple on top of the attitudinal differences that affect this issue.

Years ago I counseled a couple where the wife's chief complaint was her husband's working hours. I worked diligently with him to help him see that he could reduce his hours and not greatly affect his lifestyle. He stopped being so obsessed with his work and began to spend more time with his wife and children. Six months later the wife called for an appointment, and her new issue was that they didn't have the finances available that they did before her husband reduced his hours. "Isn't that what you wanted?" I asked. "Yes, but he still needs to make as much as he did before!" was her unrealistic reply. "Money certainly provides things that we want when we want it, but it doesn't usually make for good relationships," I responded. She was not pleased. But she had a decision to make—which was more important to her, her husband's time at home or his ability to generate more money?

You cannot have it both ways, when it comes to the hours you decide to work. My advice is to start conservatively and then increase over time if you need to make more money. And it is an issue that needs to be continually addressed over time as we grow older and our circumstances continually change. But take my advice, if you're a typical child of Western civilization, you'll tend to work too many hours, and it most likely isn't worth the price you have to pay.

step 7: learn how to be content

Everyone wants to be happy, but I submit that happiness is not the most important emotional goal. I think that contentment trumps happiness any time anywhere. Face it—there are times when it's just impossible to be happy. Parenting issues, job challenges, illnesses, and just the overall bad day. Asking people to slap a smile on their face during those times is not just difficult, it's cruel.

John and Brenda, whose story I started this chapter with, saw their finances dwindle to the point where they needed to declare bankruptcy. It was not a pleasant journey and they continued to deal with how they would provide for their children. But John decided that they would continue to focus on their marriage and he determined to take whatever work came his way so they could begin to dig their way out of their financial hole. Brenda took a part-time job that was convenient to her children's school schedule so she could pitch in. It wasn't easy, but they began, at my suggestion, to focus not on the money, but on what it would take for them to be content.

The Apostle Paul penned these words to the church in Philippi: "I know what it is to be in need, and I know what it is to have plenty. I have learned the secret of being content in any and every situation, whether well fed or hungry, whether living in plenty or in want. I can do all this through [the Lord] who gives me strength" (Philippians 4:12-13 NIV). John confided in me one session that even though he would never want to go through the turmoil of losing their wealth again, he never would have known how to be content if they had not gone through the pain of losing their money. John and Brenda learned to embrace their relative poverty, and it make their marriage stronger in the process.

[chapter 8]

go to church less

*And let us consider how we may spur one
another on toward love and good deeds,
not giving up meeting together, as some are in
the habit of doing, but encouraging one
another – and all the more as you see
the Day approaching.*

HEBREWS 10:24-25 NIV

Where I live, churches abound. They come in all sizes
and denominations, from old-line denominations stationed
in historic cathedrals to non-denominational church plants
meeting at members' houses. Going to church is no longer the
simple task of small-town America a century ago, where you
were either Protestant or Roman Catholic and your church
was chosen for you because it was the only one in town! Now,
even in small-town America, scores of church options are
beamed in daily to our televisions, and sermons once meant
for a small congregation are broadcast to millions. As a result,
the individuals or couples who are committed to a vital and
growing spiritual life have a plethora of choices from which to

choose. And our attitude toward church tends to be one of a consumer rather than a participant.

Several years ago we began to attend the church where we are now members. It was a medium-sized congregation (eight hundredmembers or so) with a dynamic young pastor at the helm. The first service I attended began with the worship leader stating these words: "Thank you for being here today and thank you for bringing the Church into this place." Now I am knowledgeable enough to know the distinction between the word "church" (small "c") and the concept of "Church" (capital "C"); the first is being the place where believers meet, the second is being the actual people that make up the Body of Believers the New Testament refers to as the Church. So, I noticed the intro, got it, and thought to myself, "That was nice." The second time I attended the same statement was made, without change, and without nuance. OK, got it. The third time—same thing. On and on it went, at every service the pastor repeated the same words! Over time my Midwestern evangelical anti-liturgical bias was beginning to set in and I became irritated: "All right, all right! Can't we be a little more creative? Original?" I was put off, mildly irritated. About the fiftieth time I attended this church, well over a year of attendance, as I sat myself down in my favorite seat on the aisle for the 9:00 AM service, I found myself mindlessly mumbling the words that began every service: "...thank you for bringing the Church into this place..." All of a sudden God spoke, and I finally got what He was trying to penetrate my heart with: "Hey Jim, stop being a consumer. Be the Church here and to a world that is in need of Me."

But what, might you might ask, does this have to do with marriage? Everything. If your faith is an important part of your life, then you will have set aside time to strengthen that faith in the context of Believers assembling themselves together to worship, be taught, and use their gifts for building each other up. But churches never "fixed" anyone, and certainly not anyone's marriage or family; God is the one who redeems and restores. The Church is just a group of people who are in this process, telling each other of God's faithfulness, and encouraging each other to continue on in the faith. It's amazing to me how easily we forget this.

* * * *

Ron and June were in my mind the quintessential church couple. Wherever they attended they immediately became involved. They sang in the choir, they taught Sunday School, they served on committees, and they were elected to leadership boards. If church attendance could guarantee a great marriage, then Ron and June would have outshone any other couple. But the truth was their marriage was awful. Both were extremely opinionated and stubborn, and when they disagreed, they became nasty and hostile. In short, their story was that they met in church as singles, immediately fell for each other and began a dating relationship that culminated in their marriage. They attended premarital classes in their church, took in a marriage preparation weekend, and were by anyone's standards fully prepared for marital life. But when they did marry, they found that their knowledge did not easily translate into actions. And over time, both accused the other of not being what they purported themselves to be in church.

"He's a hypocrite!" June exclaimed, during our first marital therapy session.

"If she thinks I'm a hypocrite, she needs to look into the mirror first!" Ron responded.

I thought this was going to be an interesting session, and it was!

June and Ron went on to relate their hope that their church would speak into their lives, or more specifically the life of their spouse.

"I met with the pastor and told him what was happening with Ron," June related to me during a session several weeks later. "I think they're shocked at how he's been treating me and I'm confident they'll be able to handle it."

Ron was incensed. "Wait until they hear from me!" he shouted. "Then they'll know the true story and who's really at fault."

"Do you really expect the church leadership to fix your marriage?" I asked.

"Yes!" they responded simultaneously. I shook my head and restated what I articulated earlier in this chapter: "The church never fixed anyone's marriage." They both looked at me as if I were a heretic, but I went on to explain that their thinking about church was not what their assumptions would have led them to believe. Ron and June suffered from misguided church expectations. Here are a few common false expectations.

false expectation #1: the church will fix my spouse, kids, and family

The Church, at its best, is a place of healing and growth. But the best any church can do is to provide an environment that promotes these things. June felt that the church leadership could fix her husband once they were aware of his faults and failures. She met with the pastor, and also demanded a meeting with the elders of the church in order to remedy the dilemma she was in. The pastor and board listened and then did what any reasonable group of people would do, they asked to speak to Ron. It probably didn't help June's cause that Ron was a member of the elder board, and when Ron was asked his side of the story, he predictably gave a completely different rendering. And so the difficulty was compounded by a process that was ineffective and by expectations that could never be met.

The belief that the church leadership can resolve conflicts is certainly biblical, and many errors of the early Church were corrected because of the corporate wisdom of the Church. But when I begin to use my local church as a place to "fix" someone else, I am putting an unjust expectation on a group of people who are attempting to follow after the example of Jesus and the early Apostles. Both Ron and June were disappointed in their church's response to their marital problems, because both of them came with the attitude that their spouse had the problems and they did not. They ended up switching churches because of their unmet expectations. Predictably, they found another church, got involved, and began to serve in leadership. They eventually repeated the same process, ending up once again disappointed with their church.

false expectation #2: the more my spouse is in church, the better he/she will become

Church attendance is a good thing, and the more time I spend in church the more I do benefit. In my decades of counseling, I am continually hearing from spouses statements like: "If only my husband/wife would come to church with me…" The implication is that we can bring our loved ones to a place where they can hear the truths of Scripture, and then they can get fixed to our specifications. My response is that the only person we need to be concerned about fixing in church is ourselves—that's why we're there, isn't it? A couple that had been working with me for years continually dealt with the issue of church. The wife was very committed to and excited with a church she had found and enthusiastically recruited her husband, who was admittedly less inclined to go to church and emphasize his spiritual life. Session after session this wife would cajole and coax and guilt her husband into joining her at church. He eventually relented, but when he would attend, he would sit and find fault with everything he could concerning the church.

When I was able to visit with the wife alone, I encouraged her to not mention church attendance any longer to her husband. She reluctantly agreed, but was skeptical about the results. Months went by, and she and the couple's son attended church faithfully without her husband. Nothing was mentioned about his attending, but one Saturday the husband finally mentioned that he'd like to accompany them the next day. When he attended of his own volition, his criticisms of the church noticeably lessened and he began to come alive spiritually. Church attendance that is coerced is not conducive to spiritual growth.

false expectation #3: the church will be the family i never had

One great benefit of being involved in a church long-term is the relationships that are built over time. When I became a believer it was delightful to call my fellow believers "brother" and "sister." I quickly settled into the joy of being someone who was encouraged and affirmed. But with these new relationships came new expectations. I now had a family that could carry me into my adult years, and the assumption was that they would be there to meet all my needs and fix my problems.

A couple I counseled years ago was involved in a very tight-knit group of committed people in a church where they attended. Their parents were part of the church as were most of their close friends. When their marriage began to experience trouble, they naturally turned to their church family for solutions. The problem was the husband had had several clandestine affairs and no one but the wife knew the details. It was a classic "he said, she said" situation. The wife, even after the affairs became known, was told to stay in a marriage with an unrepentant husband. She did, but her husband continued to lie and have affair after affair. Eventually he left and the church was silent. We spent a lengthy time dealing with her anger at the church leadership. "They were my family," she sighed to me during one session. "No they weren't," I explained. "They were your church, your spiritual brothers and sisters, and no more. Yes, you had a leadership structure in your church, but that structure isn't always perfect." She was expecting the leadership to fix something that only God could fix. They were not nor could they ever be her "new family." In the end, she was responsible for making healthy decisions, and relying on others to direct her life had been a grave mistake.

false expectation #4: the pastor and the church leadership will always be there for me

The complaint that I hear most frequently in my counseling office concerning disappointment with churches revolves around unmet expectations of pastoral performance. They usually sound something like, "I called the church to see if a pastor could see my wife's uncle in the hospital and no one ever came. We've been going to that church for ten years now and you'd think that we'd have a better response." Certainly pastoral visits are welcome during troubling times and one of the most important duties of a minister is comforting the ill and dying. But this complaint illustrates that as church members we often perpetuate a consumer mindset and not cultivate the goal of being co-laborers. I tend to view any contact that I have with a pastor outside of church itself to be a privilege not a right. Years ago my daughter was undergoing serious surgery and we were at the time in a very large church. My wife and I were pleasantly surprised when a pastor showed up to pray for my daughter right before her surgery. It was not an expectation, it was our privilege and we were blessed.

I have to mention here that most pastors are not equipped to do long-term marriage counseling. When there are urgent situations, pastors at best are urgent care counselors, stabilizing a volatile situation and directing the couple toward competent counseling. Expecting a pastor to step in and fix things is unrealistic and unfair.

In spite of what the title of this chapter might lead you to initially believe, I firmly believe that a couple's marriage is greatly enhanced by their commitment to and involvement in a local church. What I encourage couples to do when it comes to church participation would include the following:

step #1 – don't go to church until you decide to go for yourself

As I continued to work with Ron and June, I would receive regular reports of their church involvement, and a synopsis of the latest sermon. It would go something like this: "Wow, what a great message our pastor gave last weekend. It was just what Ron needed to hear. I'm waiting to see if he says anything to me about it, but I'm so glad he heard it and I hope God spoke to him." That, of course, was June's report. Ron's would go something like this: "It's great that June's at church and all, but all she does is distract. She's texting, she's fussing with the kids, and she's looking at me every time she thinks that I need to apply something to my life. June thinks that the message is for everyone but her!" During one session, in mild frustration, I asked both of them to report back to me what God told them individually during the sermon that coming weekend. "Don't think of applying it to anyone but yourself," I added. When they returned, June said that God told her to ask Ron if he was applying a certain passage of Scripture to his life. Seriously?! Ron just shook his head in frustration.

I never did quite get through to Ron and June. They were and are both delightful people and have wonderful qualities, but they could not come to a place where they were willing to look at their lives individually first, instead of trying to change each other. Church became another tool to affect their spouse rather than a place where they could be challenged and hear from God as to what He would have them change in their own lives.

step #2 – decide to serve

I have a confession to make. I am a proud man and my pride can manifest itself most disturbingly at church, of all places. I can be critical from beginning to end. Was I greeted? Was I greeted appropriately? (I want warmth, but not enthusiasm on steroids.) Can I easily find a seat on the aisle? Is the service starting on time? Is the worship appropriate? (I like contemporary—but not too loud, and not too subdued.) How's the greeting? Is the welcome given to the congregation cogent and appropriate? How's the sermon? (Total confession here: I am a sermon snob. I want my sermons concise, humorous, biblical, practical, and challenging. I want authenticity. I want vulnerability but not too much. I want a sermon that will land, not continue to fly in circles until it runs out of fuel and crashes. Is that too much to ask?!) Does the service end on time? Can I get out of the parking lot in a timely fashion? All this and I expect God to bless me for going!

When I tell couples that church would be a great place to grow together, I also tell them that when they go, they need to go with a servant's heart, not a consumer's head. I realize that church attendance is much more than just serving others, but I think it best defines the humility that's needed if two people truly want to grow as individuals and as a couple. So I am constantly asking God to help me have the heart of a servant not just in my actions but in my attitude. If your attitude is one of a servant, I can guarantee that you will maximize your worship experience both individually and as a couple.

step #3 – decide where to serve

Choosing a church is a subjective process in many ways, but I would suggest some objective handholds along the way. First, it needs to be biblical. I know that this opens up all sorts of debate and questions, but I would encourage you as a couple to simply read through The Acts of the Apostles and then use that as a template for your choice. I sincerely believe that God will give you clear direction if you agree together on this process. Second, look for a church that will teach you the Bible. Good teaching is a gift, and I believe it's necessary for spiritual growth. Third, find a church that serves the community. We attended a church that once a year had a day for single mothers. They would come to church for a delightful breakfast, hear an encouraging message, spend the rest of the morning being pampered (manicures, massages, etc.), and end with a sumptuous lunch. While two women were inside the church, the men of the church were outside washing and detailing their cars. I was proud to be part of a church that served like that. Finally, find a church that is mission-oriented. This would involve meeting the physical and spiritual needs of other countries and cultures as an act love and concern. Looking outside of ourselves is part of a healthy spiritual journey, and taking God's love to the world outside of our community helps us as we travel that road. Look for a church that has a worldwide network of servants, bringing God's love to those in need.

No church is perfect. Churches are made up of fallible, fallen people who are in the process of growing in their faith. Remember to keep a mindset of a servant and not a consumer as you consider these important factors. Jesus reminded us that if you want to be great in God's Kingdom, you must be the servant of all. It's an awesome, upside-down Kingdom!

step #4 – decide how to serve

Deciding how we serve as a couple can be tricky business. Gifting varies from individual to individual, and couples typically have different gifts from each other. One of the enjoyable aspects of marriage is the combining of individual gifts to serve together. Years ago my wife and I decided to lead a couples group with members of our church. We began to see over time how our common passions for community and spiritual growth could be addressed by combining our individual gifts. After some initial rough spots, we settled into a routine that settled itself around our gifting. I would prepare the discussion questions and study guides, and she took care of the scheduling and all the other details that enabled us to meet efficiently and comfortably.

A couple I worked with over the course of two decades has become a wonderful example of allowing their gifts to complement each other. The husband has a wonderful business sense and the ability to network and accomplish amazing things in his business. His wife has a heart for orphans worldwide and her compassion for people in need is amazing. This couple has parlayed their gifts into a ministry that is enabling orphans to be cared for and adopted into loving homes. To me, they are a beautiful example of working together to determine how they can best serve. The joy they receive in working together is indescribable.

step #5 – decide whom to serve with

I believe the backbone of any church is its ability to form and maintain small groups. I believe any church over forty people needs to relate to its parishioners on a more intimate level, and small groups are just the ticket. Over the thirty-plus years of our marriage, Renee's and my life have been defined by the people with whom we spend time. When we lived in New England our couples group helped us to create an environment of family when we had no biological family members living nearby. I would suggest four areas to talk over in terms of other couples with whom you relate. First, have a small group study; second, consider a discipleship group that would be more specific in its commitment and goals; third, a mission group for short-term mission projects state-side or overseas; and fourth, serving groups where the primary focus is to just serve other people. These are just some ideas to consider as you decide the place and people with whom you will serve.

step #6 – decide when to serve

Take your time deciding what you should do to serve the church and err on the side of doing too little as opposed to doing too much. By that I mean that it is always easier to take on more responsibility than to step down prematurely from a commitment you've made. The "80/20" rule states that 80% of the work in any volunteer organization is done by 20% of the people. Determine not to be part of that 20%. I cannot tell you the number of burnt-out people who end up feeling resentful and unappreciated in their church. I would suggest you not go down that road. My rule of thumb is if the activity feels excessively burdensome, it probably isn't the right fit for you. Work is work, but work well chosen is enjoyable and challenging. So use that as your template when you are asked to volunteer.

conclusion

So, thank you for being the Church, those of you who are believers. But your attitude toward church needs to be one of a servant and not consumer. It's OK to take your time with these decisions but I encourage you to address these issues in your marriage. My advice is to not **go** to church so much, but **be** the Church in your marriage, your family, in the world where you live, and the church where you attend. That will make not just for a better marriage but for a better life.

chapter 9

accept the fact that you're average

So, if you think you are standing firm, be careful that you don't fall! No temptation has overtaken you except what is common to mankind. And God is faithful; he will not let you be tempted beyond what you can bear. But when you are tempted, he will also provide a way out so that you can endure it.

I CORINTHIANS 10: 12-13 NIV

"I have a very serious question: are we about the most messed up married couple you've ever seen? You can be honest with us, we can take it!" This question was posed by a young wife at the end of her and her husband's first counseling session. The fact is they were fairly typical of most couples that I see. But they wanted some kind of template, some measure of how they compared to other couples and the state their marriages were in. My answer to this common question has evolved over the years into something like this: "You have serious issues to deal with, but your marriage is certainly not the worst that I've ever seen." As I delivered this statement to this young wife, she had a surprisingly disappointed look on her countenance, as if to say that if they were bad, they wanted to be "off the charts" bad.

There are many motivations for asking this question. But, generally speaking, I think there are three general reasons. The first involves the level of pain that each spouse is in. If they know that the situation is bad compared to others, then that validates the level of discomfort that they feel. Second, there is a need for some to justify abandoning their marriage. If the level of discord is deemed by a "professional source" as being extremely high, it is easier to take a step toward separation and divorce. Third, people tend not to have a good idea of what "normal" is, and when they encounter marital difficulties, they wonder if indeed they are in a relationship that is irreconcilably broken.

Chad and Cheryl had a similar question— or at least Chad did. They had been married for over twenty years and had not had a very easy time of it. Unresolved conflict, poor communication, and low-grade, pervasive anger were the constants in their marriage. During an individual session with Chad, he leaned toward me and said, "I just want a marriage like the Williams have, one where two people can continually get along without fighting." The irony of this was the fact that unbeknownst to Chad, I knew the Williams and knew their marriage was no better or worse than the one he was had with his wife. Why is it that we are so vulnerable to the "greener grass" syndrome? I believe that couples enter marriage not being aware that almost all married couples deal with similar issues, and that being prepared for challenges is half the battle.

They had difficulty understanding the need for preparation

for problems that invariably hit all married couples. They had two teenage children that were delightful and well-adjusted, but their marriage was anything but. Chronic conflict and anger had taken its toll over the years, and they had reached an impasse that was debilitating to their marriage. The frustration on their part was that they blamed each other for their difficulties, and they had unfortunately settled into a passive, non-communicative marriage. As I worked with them, we tried to normalize their situation and simultaneously minimize their feelings that they were dealing with a series of insurmountable issues. Chad was passive; Cheryl was angry. And it was obvious to me that movement was going to be difficult if we didn't first normalize their situation. Chad and Cheryl needed to embrace the fact that they were just an "average" couple, and average couples are attuned to the following realities about marriage.

reality #1:
the differences that attracted you to one another at first have a tendency to eventually become annoying.

Chad and Cheryl were attracted to each other because of their differences. Chad was shy, circumspect, and had a delightful sense of humor. Cheryl was outgoing, vivacious, and always ready with a thoughtful and informed opinion. They were an attractive couple, and enjoyed similar interests and activities. But after five years of marriage, they didn't anticipate that their differences would go from attraction to annoyance, and sometimes even reaching a point where they would attack each other. Chad's introversion went from being thoughtful to being antisocial, and Cheryl's thoughtful opinions were now considered opinionated and harsh.

reality #2:

there will always be a drama or looming drama.

When I talk to couples about the drama in their lives, I'm using that word in the sense that there will always be trouble or looming trouble in their lives. It's amazing to me how many couples are surprised when a relationship becomes difficult. Charles and Linda were married after both of their first marriages had failed. Linda brought three children into their relationship and it began with great hope and expectation. Charles would be the father that Linda's children never had, and Charles relished the idea of being the rescuing hero. But drama ensued—Linda's' children began to be critical of their step-father and went through a series of aggressive and passive-aggressive actions that put the family in turmoil. The oldest and the youngest began experimenting with drugs and the middle child was picked up for shoplifting. This drama greatly affected Charles and Linda's marriage and they found themselves moving from drama to drama with little time to work on their marriage. They became increasingly frustrated and attempted to deal with it by blaming each other. "If only he would have been more involved," Linda complained. "They wouldn't let me!" Charles responded. Even though it shouldn't have been, drama was a surprise and there was no plan in place to deal with it.

reality #3:

children will always change your marriage.

Even if children don't bring overt drama, their mere presence will bring change—usually big change. Having children is one of the biggest privileges we are afforded by God, but it is a total marriage makeover. Those beautiful babies are heavenly intruders, demanding of both parents' time and sacrifice. The second most prevalent time for divorce is seven years into the marriage, usually the time where children are now present.

Susan, an attractive professional and wife of a community leader, was a woman made for success. She was an accomplished executive and a sought after speaker, and there wasn't much that she wasn't good at. Susan wanted to have a good marriage and eventually have children. As we worked together the marriage improved due to her and her husband's hard work. She was now ready to have children and when she became pregnant, we began to prepare for the changes that having children would bring to her life. Once again, she worked hard and realistically planned for her new role.

I'll never forget the session that we had after her son was born. He was then three months old, and I looked forward to hearing the details of her new life. When the day came for the appointment, she walked into my office and literally collapsed onto the couch. "Are you OK?" I asked. She smiled and said yes and went on to say what a privilege and thrill it was to assist God in bringing a new life into the world. Then she leaned forward and said with great emphasis, "You know, Jim, I worked very hard as a professional and I prided myself in my success due to that hard work. But being a mother is absolutely the most difficult job I have ever had—I could never have imagined anything so wonderful and so daunting."

Not only did Susan's life change, so did her marriage. Communication was more difficult (no time) and doing the simplest tasks together was a challenge (no energy). "Do we have to learn to be married all over again?" was her lamenting question. I explained in more detail what she was already sensing. "Yes, you'll need to reconfigure because there's a brand new life in your family, and all relationships are changed forever." Children will change everything!

reality #4:

some spousal habits will always be annoying.

This might seem to be a minor point, but I see over and over how surprised many spouses are to discover how annoying their partner's habits have become.

Ian and Rachel had been married over twenty years but their marriage was a mess. Rachel was angry and so was Ian, but the issues were so minor that it was baffling to me what the root issues were. One of Rachel's pet peeves was Ian's habit of over-analyzing the family's orders at a restaurant. He would encourage frugality, and openly criticize any order that he deemed frivolous.

"Why would you order French fries if rice already comes with your meal?" he asked Rachel in the middle of their anniversary dinner. As she related this story to me, she said that she had reached a point that Ian's habits were literally destroying their marriage.

"I thought he would have changed by now—why doesn't he make the effort?"

Ian could only sit in silence and shrug. Finally he responded in a plaintive whine, "This never upset her before. Why is she complaining now?"

"Because I can't take it anymore!" Rachel screamed. It was clear that Ian's irritating habits were indicative of deeper issues, and Rachel began to talk about how Ian's frugality was interpreted by her as a lack of loving and honoring her. After we brought to the surface this deeper issue, I went on to suggest she could deal with Ian's habits in a more constructive way. And I asked Ian to be sensitive to anything that he was doing that annoyed Rachel, and make a genuine effort to change the offending habits. But they both needed to face the reality that people's ingrained habits rarely go away.

reality #5:

you will always deal with the tendency to live separate lives.

Intimacy is not a state of being, it is a practice that involves work and intentionality. As couples go through life together, there is a natural drifting apart that occurs in all marriages. At times couples will naturally drift together, but I find this to be much more rare and superficial in nature (doing holidays and special events together, etc.).

Bill and Terri were a perfect example. Bill's job took him all over the country selling his company's products while Terri was the mainstay at home to raising their two children. Bill was generally home on weekends, but he tended to focus on his hobbies and not his marriage or family. They eventually settled into a routine of isolation, where each did his or her own thing usually to the exclusion of the other. When I began to work with them, Terri's anger was so high that she was now threatening to leave the marriage. Both children by now had left home and they were now left to confront the fact that they had little in common.

"Why did you exclude your wife in your time at home?" I

asked Bill during one session.

"I didn't intentionally do it, I just did what I wanted to do and everything tended to be running OK in the family so I just kept on doing it. I know now how selfish I was, but I don't know if I can repair the damage."

Bill began making a concerted effort to improve their marriage, but Terri remained extremely skeptical. "I don't know if he'll ever be able to repair the damage he's done," she confided. "I don't trust that he'll ever want to put our relationship first."

Bill and Terri tried to make up for lost time, but it took Bill over two decades to realize that couples don't naturally move closer together. In reality, in the absence of intentional time together, they move farther apart.

reality #6:

you will eventually have to deal with money problems.

Money is the number one reason conflict is sparked in a marriage. I've dedicated a whole chapter on this issue in this book, but it's important for every couple to come to grips with the fact that money issues will sooner or later cause stress in a marriage relationship.

Jim and Sylvia worked together in their own business that was construction related. During the early years of the twenty-first century, they were thriving and living quite well from the proceeds of their business. When the economy crashed, so did their business. What had once been a source of pride and security, was now a broken area of their lives. They tried to manage their meager finances so they could merely survive.

"We never thought we'd ever have to really worry about

making ends meet," Jim told me. "Our lives are now day-to-day, job-to-job, and paycheck-to-paycheck. It's caught us completely off guard."

"He's become a miser," Sylvia intoned. "There's not a day that goes by that he doesn't complain that I'm spending too much or unwisely. He's become unbearable!"

Every couple, while perhaps not going through the severe loss of wealth that Jim and Sylvia went through, will deal with the difficulties of money availability and money management.

reality #7:

you will have issues concerning your professions and work schedules.

My wife Renee and I have dealt with my profession and work schedule on and off our whole married life. These issues have grown in intensity over the past two decades of our marriage. My profession is time intensive and quite stressful, and her profession is worldwide in scope and includes times of lengthy travel. Our conflicts tend to revolve around the time that I spend at work, and the "appointment creep" that happens to my schedule on a regular basis. "You didn't tell me that you would be working so long on Saturday," is an often-heard statement from my wife to me. My response, reasoned and compelling, is completely lost on my wife because she's able to see through the fog of my rationalizations. I'm fudging on my promises to spend time with my wife for reasons that I find compelling, but my wife does not. Just the time that we think that we have all the bases covered on this issue, something out of the ordinary happens—something that I deem compelling and Renee regards as not as important. Average marriages deal with professional and work schedule issues continually, and take it from me, they really don't go away!

reality #8:

differences in parenting styles will always challenge your marriage.

Pete and Margot had a great marriage, except when it came to parenting. Two totally different life experiences compounded by gender differences conspired to continually rob their marriage of the peace that they both desired. Their oldest child, a son, was a typical first-born: a high-achiever, and a rule follower. But when he entered high school he began to falter both academically and spiritually by his mother's estimation. Margot immediately clamped down and held him accountable for his time at home when he wasn't at school. She was determined that he bring up his grades and that he spend the appropriate time building his spiritual life.

Pete saw his role completely different as his son's parent. He wanted to talk through the issues and then give his son room to adjust his life to make the appropriate choices. Who was correct?

"I think Pete is being negligent in his role as a parent," exclaimed Margot, "If he continues to coddle our son, then we'll have a real mess on our hands."

"Margot doesn't understand boys and she certainly doesn't understand our son. If she continues to micro-manage him, he will shut down and then we'll have a real mess on our hands," Pete responded.

So who was right? What Pete and Margot didn't account for was the differences in parenting styles can pose a threat to the marital relationship. They asked me who was right, and I refused to choose one over the other (vote for me!). What I did say was that their son needed both of their points of view and their unity in a plan to deal with his current situation. Average marriages always deal with parenting issues.

In looking at these challenging realities, the issue initially for married couples is not how to fix these problems, but to view them first of all as normative. Too many couples are surprised at adversity, and they assume that if they've made a good choice for a spouse that problems won't come their way as they do for couples, or perhaps as they did for their parents in their families of origin. This couldn't be further from the truth. Conflict is common to all marriages (as you can see in the chapter on conflict) and thinking that something is wrong with your marriage because you encounter any or all of these realities is just wrong thinking. So the challenge is not to avoid these realities, but to deal with them in a productive and healthy manner. As we deal with the responsibilities of being the spouses that we truly desire to be, I would suggest the following antidotes to help couples excel at being average.

how to deal with being average in an above-average manner

antidote number one: expect attack

Tom and Adrienne had come to me for pre-marital counseling. We went through several sessions to discover some of the issues that they would confront in their first years of marriage. During their last session a few weeks before their wedding I congratulated them for their work and then reminded them that there were tough times to come. I warned them that there will be attacks down the road. Wide-eyed and optimistic, they said that they would be ready.

Three months after their wedding, Tom and Adrienne were back in my office.

"I had no idea that it would be such an adjustment," Adrienne said. "We thought that the fact that we loved each other so much would take care of most everything. Why didn't you tell us that it would be such an adjustment on so many fronts?"

"She's not very nice when she's upset," Tom added. "You did tell us that we'd have a tough time but we never expected anything like this." We worked through the difficulties and they got back on track, but Tom and Adrienne understood a bit better that things were not going to always be easy.

Expecting attack is not just a mental awareness, it is an activity. For couples with a strong faith, the words of Jesus come resounding through the centuries: "In this world you will have trouble. But take heart, I have overcome the world" (John 16:33 NIV). Being on the alert for attack will accomplish two things. First, you will not lose time wondering if something is wrong with your marriage. Second, you can move on to your plan.

antidote number two: have a plan

I am not a natural planner. In fact, my wife puts me to shame in this category. Her whole life is planned out and time is used wisely and expeditiously. Plans and I don't naturally get along. But since I've owned my own business, I've been forced to plan if I want it to be successful. So I guess if I have to do what it takes to plan, it's possible. But planning for my marriage is another thing altogether.

When I encourage couples to plan, I try to make it as simple as possible, mainly because I am instructing out of my own personal need. The focus is in two primary areas: time and activities. First, it takes time to work together and plan how to do life. Plans don't just show up on our doorsteps; they are forged in moments of focused communication. This is what I suggest:

time:

one-on-one time for fifteen minutes every day. These times need to be totally focused spouse to spouse and require an environment where you will not be interrupted.

one hour per week planning time. Couples can use this time to coordinate schedules and make decisions concerning events that are upcoming.

one evening per week. Use this time to relax and enjoy each other. I suggest that these times not be used for any heavy discussions or serous conflict. Have fun together!

one weekend per quarter. This is certainly more difficult for couples who are on a tight budget, but use your creativity to assure you can spend extended time together away from your house and, if you have them, children. These times can be used for long-term planning and processing major decisions you might have.

Many times when I suggest these time parameters with couples, I'm met with stares and open mouths. "How will we ever find the time to do that?" is the common rejoinder. I usually respond by saying that you will always find time to do the things that you want to do, and suggest that they encourage each other to build their schedules around prearranged times to talk and plan.

focus:

spiritual. Being intentional about how you are going to grow closer to God as a couple is a non-negotiable. This would include church involvement and how you want to encourage each other as a couple. Prayer together is an excellent way to grow closer as a couple.

marital. How will you work on your marriage as you grow older together? Issues such as communication, conflict resolution, mutual trust, and marital satisfaction should be discussed regularly. What resources will you use to enhance your relationship? If you are "stuck," where will you go to find help? It's important to have an agreement as to how you will address issues that are not easily resolved.

financial. Determine how you want to manage your money. Come up with a budget together and determine who will have what responsibilities in paying bills and making sure the boundaries of the budget are kept. The budget should be examined and evaluated once per month.

professional. Talk through your goals and expectations for work. How many hours per week will you commit to? Will just one of you work or will you both work? What goals do you have for your advancement or further education? It's important to talk through your expectations ahead of time, so you'll be able to make informed decisions when your employment situation changes.

recreational. Discuss what will you plan to do together to enhance your life and just have fun together. What areas do you want to explore together? And how much time will you commit to recreational activities? Vacation times and locations should be discussed as well.

empty nest/retirement. Even though this might be one or two decades away, plan for when your children will leave home and what you will do when that happens. What will you do differently? Will you move or look to purchase a second home? What areas of personal development will become available to you during this time? Use this time to dream and be intentional about what finance and professional issues will need to be addressed.

parenting. What goals will you establish for your children? Use parenting resources to establish how you want to raise your children and what boundaries you wish to give them. Also, because each child is different, how will you go about adjusting your parenting to meet the needs of each child.

*   *   *   *

Chad and Cheryl, after having worked through their disappointment with each other, needed to get to a place where they stopped the comparison game. But how do you arrive at the point where you stop looking at others and focus on your own marriage? The simple answer is that you choose to focus on what you have and what you can do personally to change your situation. A life spent comparing and coveting is a life that is absolutely wasted. When Chad and Cheryl stopped looking over their shoulders at other marriages they were then able to concentrate on what their personal responsibilities were to make their marriage work. Finally, during a session, Chad looked at Cheryl and said, "I want to make our marriage work, not worry that our marriage isn't as good as other marriages."

Chad and Cheryl realized finally that they were average— not average in a sense that they were not gifted people and their marriage not capable of excellence, but average in the sense that everything that they were experiencing was not abnormal but quite common to all marriages. As King Solomon so wisely proclaimed, "There is nothing new under the sun." By embracing the normalcy of their challenges, Chad and Cheryl finally became better equipped to deal with the problems they were facing.

[chapter 10]

be less religious

Why do you look at the speck of sawdust in your brother's eye and pay no attention to the plank in your own eye? How can you say to your brother, 'Let me take the speck out of your eye,' when all the time there is a plank in your own eye? You hypocrite, first take the plank out of your own eye, and then you will see clearly to remove the speck from your brother's eye.

MATTHEW 7: 3-5 NIV

Jerry and Ann came to see me with a deeply troubled marriage. Jerry was in full-time Christian ministry and Ann worked in a secular profession. Jerry was extremely gifted and had pastored a church that was the fastest-growing congregation in their community. He was respected and loved by his parishioners, but not so much by his wife. Jerry had an anger problem which was exacerbated by his tendency to imbibe alcohol to "blow off some steam." To counter her husband's dysfunctional behavior, Ann had turned negative and cynical in her interactions with Jerry, and she continually complained of his inappropriate and disruptive behavior. Their marriage had disintegrated into a series of intense arguments augmented by periods of sullen calm. At best Jerry and Ann tolerated each other and at worst their mutual feelings had sunk to the level of loathing.

When I asked what Jerry wanted in his marriage, his first answer was a supportive wife. I thought this was a reasonable expectation, providing, of course, he was also being supportive to her. When I asked Ann what she wanted in a husband, she said she wanted Jerry to love her unconditionally and not let his anger get out of control.

No sooner were these words out of her mouth than Jerry lashed out, "I suppose the only person you'd be really happy with is Jesus himself. Well, I'm NOT Jesus! In fact," he went on to say, "until you do what the Bible tells you to do, I don't think you deserve anything at all."

"And what is it that the Bible is telling her to do?" I queried.

"You know... she should submit to me in all things and not always push back and be so negative to my leadership and ideas. And," he added, "she should have sex with me more often."

I correctly ascertained at this point that this was not going to be a very fun session. The rest of the session was a game of "biblical gotcha," with each quoting passages that were aimed at changing each other's behavior. During the last five minutes, Ann turned to me in frustration and said, "Why aren't you saying anything? Who's right and who's wrong in this discussion?"

After a bit of a pause, I said, "You're not going to like my answer, but in my opinion, you're both wrong. You're trying to change each other by pointing out the error of his or her ways."

Since they were throwing around Scripture right and left, I thought I might as well throw in one of my own. I quoted the text from Matthew 7, suggesting that they attend to the planks in their own eyes before they continue prosecuting one another. "You're both so caught up with trying to point out each other's failures that you cannot see where you're failing yourselves." They both looked at me and neither one responded. I got the impression they didn't like my choice of Scripture.

Ann and Jerry were both well-meaning Christians; they both sincerely believed that they knew what God wanted their marriage to be. The problem was that their commitment to faith and biblical knowledge was used against their spouse instead turning inward toward changing themselves. There are common stumbling blocks to marriages where one or both spouses are committed to living their lives by biblical principles. These attitudes are summed up in the following statements, which though are sometimes directly stated, more often they are implied:

"i am better than you."

Geoff and Cindy booked an appointment for marriage therapy and when they came, Cindy began to enumerate their problems while Geoff glumly sat and listened. "He's angry all the time, he doesn't listen, and he's totally selfish!" she said. "And furthermore, he doesn't participate in church activities and is distant from our children." "What do you have to say to that?" I asked Geoff. "Nothing except I think she's exaggerating my bad qualities," he mumbled. Over the course of the session it became obvious to me that Geoff was not doing a very good job in his role as a husband. Cindy, however, wasn't doing all that much better in her role as a wife. Yet everything she said and the tone in which she said it shouted out her conviction that she was indeed superior to her husband. "So you're telling me that you are better than your husband?" I asked her. For the first time during the session she hesitated.

As a Christian, she knew that this was a curveball question. If she answered yes, then she would be guilty of pride, but if she answered no, then she would lose the leverage of her argument. She finally said, "Well, nobody is better than anyone else, I guess, but when people do bad things, it sure doesn't make them fun to be around." "So you are better than Geoff," I persisted. "I didn't say that..." she began to say. "You say you're better than me every day of our married life," Geoff interjected. Finally, Geoff was speaking! They began to go back and forth for a bit until I asked Geoff, "So are you better than Cindy?" "Not really, but at least I don't badger her and tell her how much of a disappointment she is," Geoff said. "So you are better than Cindy," I said. Now both Geoff and Cindy were frustrated—with me! They were caught up in a debilitating interaction of comparison. Every one of us has the natural inclination to compare ourselves to others. And we usually come out pretty good in the process, at least in our own minds. I went on to give them the best advice I could to help, the antireligious correction:

"we are all equal in the sight of God."

When I made this statement, both Geoff and Cindy looked at me with mild irritation. No person of faith would disagree with this statement, but living it out is not so easily done. Finally Cindy responded, "We know that. That's not going to fix this mess!" "I'm not saying it will," I countered, "but if you don't start here, you'll get nowhere in your marriage and your ability to communicate and resolve conflict." Religion by its very nature declares itself as truthful, and thus, everyone else is false. Now I do believe in absolute truth and that when you don't live in truth, bad things happen. But using religion as a weapon is antithetical to what God wishes to do in our lives and our relationships. For Christians, there is only one Person with whom we compare ourselves, and that's Christ Himself. This truth doesn't ignore our faults and failures, it just allows us the ability to have a positive discussion concerning what a healthy marriage looks like.

"i am right and you are wrong."

Harry and Dina were barely hanging on when it came to their twenty-three-year marriage. They had met in college and had dated a year when they decided to marry. The problem that became evident early on in their marital life was that they were going in two totally different directions spiritually. When Dina first met Harry, he had a strong faith and was quite zealous in his wanting to grow as a Christian. Dina admired his consistency and self-denial and looked forward to a relationship where they both could encourage each other to continue to grow. But after their wedding, Harry experienced a series of setbacks and frustrations both personally and professionally. He became angry and embittered, and soon began to drift away from his spiritual commitments. Dina, on the other hand, began to find joy and comfort in her relationship with God and as she and Harry drifted apart, she relied more and more on God and her church family.

After more than two decades of this drift, Dina had had enough. She increasingly pointed out how Harry was failing in his personal life and in his relationship with his wife and children. Our sessions consisted of a listing of Harry's shortcomings, and his unwillingness to change and move in a more positive direction. During our third session together, Dina looked at him during a heated exchange and said, "Face it, Harry. I'm right and you're wrong. I'm walking with God and you're not. So you better start seeing things the right way, or this marriage is going to end." Now to be honest, Dina had legitimate complaints about Harry and his unwillingness to change. But my response to Dina was given to her the next time we had a one-on-one session. "Do you really think you're always right and that Harry's always wrong?" "Well," she responded, "I certainly am the one who is trying to obey God and to follow Scripture. Of course I'm in the right—God is perfect and His Word is a perfect guide for our lives." "But do you follow His path perfectly, Dina?" I asked. "No, but that doesn't mean that Harry's right and I'm wrong," she answered. I went on to state what I felt was the best stand to take on this situation:

"only God is right 100% of the time."

I told Dina that while I greatly respected her faith and how she was living it out, she needed to not fight the fight of "right and wrong" and own her missteps rather than going on a mission to prove Harry wrong. Even though she had legitimate issues with how he was behaving, she was fighting a battle that she would never win, and her actions were putting her in a position that was Pharisaical. At first she tried to convince me that I was wrong (!) but over time gave up the fight to prove to her husband how wrong he was. And as she did this, lo and behold, Harry began to see his faults much more clearly.

God blesses me but he does not (cannot) bless you.

The original sin was not that of Adam and Eve. The original sin was conjured up by a mighty supernatural being that dared to be equal to God. Lucifer was an angel of the highest degree, a being of beauty and majesty. What was he thinking?! Why would he ever put himself in a place where he knew he could never be? I believe it was the desire for just a bit more, a blessing that would make him just a bit more special. And we as human beings are certainly no better. In my earlier days as a Christian, I labored under the gross misconception that now that I was a believer, God would not only bless me more, but He would bless everything I did. It was a great way to live except for one thing: it was not biblical!

Many times, a spouse's shortcomings are used as a screen for our own issues. For example, if a husband has a drinking problem, then that dysfunction can become an unhealthy cover for the wife's issues and deflect her from addressing her own shortcomings. And the great temptation is that the "healthy" spouse plays the role of God. When bad things happen to the offending spouse, there is an attitude of "I told you so" that serves no purpose other than to give one spouse a false sense of victory and humiliate the other spouse. The reality is that it only serves to drive them apart.

"God blesses those whom He chooses, irrespective of anyone's opinion of whether it's deserved or not."

A wife using her husband's shortcomings to obfuscate her own dysfunctions in the marriage leads both spouses to isolation. It puts her in the position of secretly rooting for her husband to fail, even though she outwardly complains to him when he falls short of her expectations. She runs the danger of allowing herself to be distracted by her own faulty interpretation of how God deals with individuals. Jesus said that God allows the sun to shine and the rain to fall on the righteous and the unrighteous. The Psalms are filled with complaining to God that the evil flourish while the righteous suffer. But the ultimate answer to that lament is that God is in charge of all the affairs of man, and playing the comparison game leads to nothing but frustration. Excessive religiosity is the death knell of such relationships.

"i am able to be your judge."

Karla had a drinking problem. This fact was not initially evident to me, however. Karla was a vivacious, attractive professional, and was a married mother of two children. What was evident to me was that Karla didn't get along with her husband at all. Doug was also a successful professional who had a reputation for hard work along with integrity. But Doug had an anger problem. This fact was also not initially evident to me. I became aware of Doug and Karla's issues via the "squeal method." Both of them ratted each other out, and did it with great drama and panache. Their marriage had turned into a standoff where each of them had staked out a positions on why the other was at fault for their troubled marriage.

Our sessions consisted of extremes: there were declarations of love and commitment juxtaposed with indictments of character and blame. I had the unenviable task of counseling two "judgers." It was not a fun experience. "His anger is totally out of control!" Karla exclaimed. And as she detailed Doug's rages, I felt she was correct in her assessment. Over time, he validated the anger label by being furious with Karla during a session because she didn't want to coordinate her schedule to come in with him. He was furious with her selfishness! He made the mistake of asking me if I would have been mad at my wife if the same thing happened to me—he wasn't pleased with my answer. Karla couldn't help but smile. "See, I told you so!" she exulted. "But I also can tell you that if you were my wife, I wouldn't be comfortable with the amount that you're drinking," I responded. Karla's exultation was short-lived. "I don't drink that much," she said, defensively. All this produced in Doug was a profound rolling of his eyes.

"only God is our judge."

Both Doug and Karla had tried the other in the courtroom of their minds and had convicted each other on any and all charges. And even though both claimed to be committed followers of Christ, they seemed to have forgotten His exhortation to "judge not, lest you too be judged." Jesus is not asking us to be morally neutral, he is commanding us to make sure we never usurp God's role and make it our own. Judgment is not mentioned at all in our job descriptions! Doug and Karla overlooked this admonition to their marital peril. As they began to see this, they also began to back off from their harsh words toward each other. I'm glad to say that Doug decided to be the husband he was supposed to be while simultaneously putting Karla's faults on the back burner. As he remained consistent in doing this, his anger subsided and Karla began to look more clearly at her addiction. She decided not to drink any longer and they are today enjoying a healthy and satisfying marriage relationship. And they don't have to carry the extra burden of being each other's judge!

"if we have conflict, you are at fault."

No one, I believe, really likes conflict. Some may handle it better than others, but I don't think that anyone wants conflict to be a constant part of marriage. I've devoted a whole chapter on conflict, but I wanted to mention one of the biggest impediments to conflict resolution in the context of this chapter. Recently a couple came to see me saying they needed immediate intervention. The issue in essence was a pattern of chronic conflict they had fallen into that had been happening for over five years. Overall, their relationship was excellent. They loved each other and were mutually supportive. But the unresolved conflict was wearing them down and their marriage was in a chronically painful state. "She brings things up just to be combative," the husband complained. "She just doesn't realize how wrong she is to hang on to issues that just aren't that important." When I talked with the wife , her complaint was her husband was initially angry in the conflicts and then would withdraw from their relationship. "He gets angry and then disappears," she complained. As it turned out, husband and wife were both classic conflict avoiders.

When they showed up at my office, their situation had not improved. They actually showed little willingness to change their positions throughout most of our extended time together. Finally, more out of frustration than therapeutic skill, I asked them both, "OK, who's right and who's wrong?" The couple were both silenced by the question. They were both committed Christians so they recognized that it was a loaded question. For one spouse to say overtly that he or she was right and the other wrong was to risk sounding prideful and arrogant. But to admit to being wrong was to lose the whole point of the conflict. I went on to say, "If you are assuming that your spouse is wrong (or unreasonable, or mistaken, or misguided—whatever adjective you want to use), then you will not be able to resolve any conflict n a healthy and edifying manner. Listen to each other and mirror back what you are hearing. Then, attempt to isolate your contribution to the disagreement so you can adjust accordingly." I was attempting to communicate this solution to their problems:

"i could just as easily be at fault as you."

This couple, in their effort to live beyond the conflict they were experiencing, refused to hear each other and to own their responsibility for the conflict. Later on, they both admitted that they already knew the truth of what I was saying, but they didn't realize that they were not living up to what they believed. As they resisted their propensity to assume the other was wrong, they were better able to hear each other, and that enabled them to begin to get out of their chronic cycle of conflict. I don't think I've ever seen such a remarkable turnaround in a couple, and they continue to work toward a more intimate relationship.

"you need to change."

I am trained in systems therapy, more commonly known as marriage and family therapy. One of the foundational principles in this therapeutic model is that for a relationship of a family to deal with chronic problems, change must be injected into the family or marital system. The problem with this concept is that human nature puts us in a place where we expect others to change if we are going to change, and in more extreme circumstances, we expect others to change first. A good place to start is to determine to show your spouse kindness on a consistent basis. Clients will often look at me with a "And I'm paying for this?" attitude when I suggest kindness as a change agent, but simple kindness can begin a healing process that can change a relationship for the better.

"instead of expecting my spouse to change, i need to change first."

This is the whole point of Jesus' admonition to "take the plank out of your own eye." We need to see to ourselves first, before we expect others to change. And the amount of change is not something we need to measure. I am often asked, "How much longer do I need to focus on my own change before I focus on my spouse?" My answer is the same for all my clients: "Just give me one more day, and one more day after that…" When individuals embrace this concept, it puts them in a healthier position to love and be loved.

Jerry and Ann, the couple with which we began this chapter, were never able to get beyond their own expectations of each other. Their marriage didn't end, but their intimacy continued to decline because they kept looking to each other to change in order to save the marriage. Their religious convictions, instead of moving them toward each other were used as reasons to blame each other. The outside shell of their marriage was intact, but the inside was sadly rotting away. Their faith compelled them to not divorce, but it didn't take them to a place of genuine repentance and reconciliation. Personal faith is vital for personal growth, but that faith needs to be directed in one direction: toward yourself and not your spouse!

chapter 11

give up finding your soulmate

If you have any encouragement from being united with Christ, if any comfort from his love, if any common sharing in the Spirit, if any tenderness and compassion, then make my joy complete by being like-minded, having the same love, being one in spirit and of one mind. Do nothing out of selfish ambition or vain conceit. Rather, in humility value others above yourselves not looking to your own interests, but each of you to the interests of others. In your relationships with one another, have the same mindset as Christ Jesus..

PHILIPPIANS 2: 1-5 NIV

Joe and Diane were what appeared to be a normal couple with a marriage that had lasted well over three decades. They had raised four children, worked faithfully at their jobs in the medical field, and retired early. They were compatible, adventurous, and for their age were extremely active. No casual observer would ever guess that their marriage was hanging by a thread. And the reason? Facebook.

Well, not actually Facebook, but what Facebook enabled Joe to do. One year before I first met with them, Joe had researched and contacted an old girlfriend from his college days. This had been Joe's first serious relationship. It broke up suddenly, and left him with an emotionally painful void in his life. For years, even after he met and married Diane, Joe had wondered why the relationship ended. You can imagine what happened next: Joe contacted his old girlfriend, they "caught up," and even though both were married, they began to rekindle an intimate relationship. This, of course, caused Joe to emotionally distance himself from Diane. She became confused and her in anger grew at his aloof attitude. Inevitably, Diane discovered Joe's secret, tipped off when he ran up an excessive phone bill. She wanted to know why over three hundred phone calls had been made to Joe's hometown in a period of three months. After some prodding, Joe finally told Diane that he had contacted his old flame. As is typical in such situations, he minimized both his actions and his emotional involvement. But slowly, over the period of a few weeks, the truth came out that he was involved in an emotional affair. It was at this time that they came to my office for counseling.

Joe and Diane's situation is unfortunately typical. I have often wondered how it is that couples like them, with years of marriage and building a life together, could end up so far apart emotionally and and in such a hurtful manner to one another (in this case by Joe). Diane was distraught and determined to do what she could to repair their marriage, but Joe's attitude could be summed up in a statement he made to me during one of our one-on-one sessions: "This woman I dated in college was my first love, and I know now that she was my one and only true love. I'll never be able to love another like her." This realization included the convinction that he would not be able to love his wife of thirty-plus years and the mother of their four children. I had to fight off a strong gag reflex upon hearing those words. Not that Joe was a bad man; he was just spectacularly and tragically misguided.

What is it that causes couples like Joe and Diane to come to such a difficult place in their relationship? In the course of doing marriage therapy, I consistently hear the following statements, or ones similar to them:

> "I am not married because I haven't found my soulmate yet."

> "My first marriage was nothing but trouble, but now I've found my soulmate."

> "I love my spouse, but I'm not 'in love' with my spouse."

> "My spouse will never be my soulmate."

> "We were soulmates early in our relationship, but that's just not the case anymore."

Of all the mistaken concepts foisted on the American culture over the last century, the concept of finding your soulmate is perhaps the greatest destroyer of marriages. I realize that Hollywood has been a convenient scapegoat for all sorts of disgruntled people, but I have to put a good portion of the "in love" myth squarely on its shoulders. The whole process of "falling in love" is one of the most coveted experiences in our culture; the harsh reality is that falling in love is no more than a temporary excitement that comes with a new relationship.

This excitement is sustained by unusually high activity of our hormones and often complemented by a propensity to live in fantasy.

I'm often asked by young couples in pre-marital counseling about compatibility. "Shouldn't our interests be the same?" "Shouldn't our personalities be similar?" "What should we have as goals in common?" Questions like these are pertinent and worthy of consideration. I'm convinced, after thousands of hours of counseling couples, compatibility is something you create, not something you find. It's my experience that the more a couple is different in personality traits, the healthier the marriage can potentially become. The work that causes a relationship to move in a healthy direction focuses on communication and conflict resolution with a view toward building a future together with shared dreams and goals. The emotions that come with new relationships always fade over time, and can become a false barometer of the health of a relationship.

We are an emotional culture and there really is nothing inherently wrong in that. But it can lead to being caught up in relational myths that consistently work against a couple having a successful and satisfying marriage. Here are some of the misguided statements that I hear regularly around the topic of soulmates:

myth #1: "i missed my soulmate"

Joe and Diane, while outwardly civil toward each other, were angry and disillusioned with each other. Their marriage was an up-and-down relationship with more downs than ups. Conflict, lack of communication, and a complete lack of trust permeated their lives, and they were both fed up. When Joe finally told me his story, his chief lament was that he had made a second-best choice when he married. "I didn't marry my true love," he mourned, and after a longer pause he wistfully whispered, "I missed my soulmate."

Really! It's as if our journey through this life is a search for "the one," the only person that is uniquely suited to join us in our life's journey so we can be completely fulfilled and happy. And if we can just be diligent enough, or patient enough, or wise enough, then we will be truly completed. And God help me if I miss "the one." If I do, then I will be consigned to a life of mediocrity at best, and abject misery at worst. Not only is this not true, it is a dangerous and nefarious lie. Any man and woman, if completely committed and focused, can have a growing and mutually satisfying relationship. Finding a soulmate has nothing to do with it.

myth #2: "i fell out of love with him/her"

This is a statement that is uttered in my office on a regular basis. It is often delivered in a softer version: "I love my husband/wife, but I am not 'in love' with him/her." Someday, in complete frustration and agony, I will blurt out what I really think about that statement. It will go something like: "That is absolute hogwash!" But right now I am still able to stifle myself and struggle along with, "Tell me what you mean by that." The problem is I already know what they mean. They are trying to tell me that the emotional component of their marriage is in bad shape, and they aren't very happy about it. And, in fact, they are trying to use that reasoning to justify the contemplation of leaving their marriage.

Joe and Diane had come to me struggling with their marriage.

Financial hardships and poor communication were two issues that they hadn't anticipated in the later years of their marriage. They were an attractive couple, and there was no reason that I could think of that they shouldn't enjoy their relationship. But one session Joe stated that he didn't think that he was in love with his wife any longer. "Tell me what being 'in love' means," I said. His quizzical look told me that he not only didn't like my question, but was questioning my competence as a counselor. "You know what I mean!" he exclaimed. "I really don't," was my rejoinder. "But," I continued, "I think I can guess. You mean that you no longer feel for Diane what you once felt for her. And try as you might, you cannot get that feeling back. And the more you spend time together, the more you are irritated and frustrated with the fact that she just doesn't seem to connect with you emotionally like she did earlier on in your relationship, especially when you were dating. You're also telling me that you are seriously contemplating ending the marriage with the primary reason being that you just aren't in love with Diane any longer. How am I doing?"

"Well," he responded, "I wouldn't put it quite that bluntly, but yes, I guess that about sums it up." "Who told you that you needed to be 'in love' to be married?" I asked. "Everyone sort of assumes that, don't they?" he said, with a puzzled look. I believe that Joe's view of relationships is originated in a Hollywood fantasy that has been foisted on our culture for at least one hundred years. Everyone likes falling in love. It's fun, it's exciting, and it has the wonderful feature of not seeming like it requires any effort at all. In fact, being in love is what life and relationships are all about, right? Wrong! Scientists tell us the feelings of being in love last anywhere from six hours to sixteen months. But after that, I guess it's a little tougher, right? Right! Joe wasn't happy, but being in love had little to do with his state of being. How he responded to the challenges in his relationship with Diane had much more to do with his attitude toward her and their marriage.

Myth #3: "we've grown apart"

Take a look at that statement and analyze it with me for a second, if you would. What strikes you about it? Does it affect you the same as it affects me? Of all the self-contradictory statements anyone could make, this would have to rank near the top if not the number one example. How do you "grow apart"? I assume that this is a large part of what Joe and Diane were trying to convey to me. "But is this growth?" I asked. "Is where you are individually better than where you were?" Both had to admit that they were not growing at all. "So maybe a better way to say it is that you've drifted apart due to your lack of attention to each other and to the marriage," I suggested. After a bit of a disgruntled pause, both had to agree. "That's such a negative way to put it," Diane said, "and I don't like the way that sounds." I wanted to say that I didn't like what they had allowed their relationship to become, but I resisted!

"We've grown apart" is an oxymoron of the first order. There is no "growth" when the result is relational distance. Joe and Diane were reaping the results of years of benign neglect to their marriage. Joe was successful in his business and the family enjoyed an excellent standard of living. Diane was focused on their children but she also had a successful career. But when the money became less abundant due to a job change, they found themselves in a relationship with no visible signs of health. And to top that off, they began to blame each other for their predicament, but both were culpable. Our culture had tolerated similar excuses when it comes to human behavior. The student who has just flunked out of college says, "I just lost interest in being in school," or the worker who has just been fired says, "I didn't feel that the job matched my gifting and interests." Certainly people do lose interest in school, and jobs don't always fit, but to use these as reasons for a lack of effort and negligence is just not being honest.

Joe and Diane needed to start with a different premise and to change their goal. The premise that is more accurate is "Through our mutual neglect we have grown apart," and their goal needed to be doing whatever it took to becoming intimate again, becoming "one flesh." The years of not working on their marriage, not communicating, not working through conflicts had established a pattern of resentment and neglect. Diane finally began to see this and to work at communicating more effectively. Joe, on the other hand, refused to give his relationship with Diane the 100% effort that it demanded. He refused to let go of the soulmate myth.

myth #4: "my only true love was my first love"

Of all the myths that I've listed, this is probably the most difficult one to deal with because like any other effective lie, there is a bit of truth in it. It is true that there is nothing like your first love, because of the simple fact that the initial experience can never be duplicated. And like any other enjoyable experience, its true essence usually exaggerated with time. The reality of our past is warped by our present longings.

Joe was convinced, or better put, had convinced himself that his only chance at "true love" was rekindling his relationship with his first love. He struggled to focus on his marriage, but in spite of his promises and reassurances to his wife, he continued to contact this other woman, who in fact was also married. Try as I might, I was not able to convince him that the wife and children he presently had were worth the work he needed to do to restore his marriage. He lived in a fantasy that he just wouldn't give up. Instead of dealing with his present unhappiness and doing what he needed to do to be the husband that his wife needed, Joe chose to live in a newly created world where he could leave his troubles and shortcomings behind and enjoy true joy and happiness. The problem was and still is that you cannot leave **yourself** behind. Your true self tends to eventually show up in every new relationship you create, and the problems will always repeat themselves.

Joe left and didn't come back for a while, until seven months down the road he realized that there were things that he couldn't escape and issues that he couldn't deal with even in an idealized relationship. He came home to Diane with humility and genuine repentance, and she graciously, with clearly formed boundaries, took him back. They are still working on renewing their marriage and it is very hard work indeed. But it is work that is no longer impeded by the "first love" myth.

myth #5: "i need to go from relationship to relationship until i find my soulmate"

This myth is unfortunately the most destructive of all. It is based on the false premise that "the One" is somewhere out there and it's up to us to keep trying until we find him or her. A few years back there was a book written entitled *The Starter*

Marriage in which the author chronicles the sociological trend of people marrying and then divorcing after a period of no more than seven years, all with the purpose of finding a more suitable spouse. The reasoning is that since we don't know ourselves that well, let alone other people, we need to try multiple relationships in order for us to know what truly will make us happy.

Keith and Debbie, married eighteen years, came into my office with a problem. Well, really only Debbie had a problem, and Keith was a bit clueless. I was presented with a list of offenses for which Keith was responsible, and I listened with interest as his wife then proceeded with the aid of her own copy, to read off her many complaints. To be honest, the complaints were not what I would consider to be in the serious category. In fact, I thought that the complaints were common ones, more in the category of knuckleheaded. I came to this conclusion because Debbie's complaints were ones my wife has about my functioning as a husband. They included a lack of involvement in household chores, relational insensitivities like being late or missing the mark celebrating an important event—you know, pretty much any husband's normal MO. But Debbie was really mad, and it took me quite a while to figure it out—and actually Keith figured it out, not me.

Debbie's main complaint, when all was said and done, was that Keith was not her soulmate. We addressed their emotional intimacy issues, Keith's taking on more responsibility for the household and parenting, and Keith's sensitivity to putting his wife first and not his family of origin. When Keith stepped up in all these categories, Debbie became even angrier and more dissatisfied. And that's when I knew we had trouble. I asked Keith if he thought his wife was perhaps having an affair.

He was shocked at the question, and insisted that there was no indication. Eventually Debbie asked for a separation and then a divorce. It was only after the divorce that Keith found out that his wife had had several affairs during their marriage, and that she had done this in an attempt to find her one true love. Needless to say, Debbie's search ended in disappointment and continued bitterness, and even though Keith was willing to forgive her, he could do nothing to convince his ex-wife to come back to the marriage. She just couldn't give up the idea that the perfect person was out there, somewhere, and she just needed to keep looking.

combatting the myths

In order to effectively counteract the myths surrounding the concept of a soulmate, I encourage couples to consider and then be reminded of the following truths:

the cultural concept of finding a soulmate is indeed a myth

The first step in debunking a myth is to recognize it as one. There are two popular romantic comedies that illustrate this quite clearly: *Sleepless in Seattle* and *You've Got Mail*, both starring Tom Hanks and Meg Ryan. Now in the interest of full disclosure, I think Tom Hanks is a very good actor, if not one of the best today. And Meg Ryan—well, she's cute! Both movies revolve around the soulmate myth and a romanticized view of relationships. The tension builds in both movies as the audience wonders if the two lovers (and truly wonderful people!) will ever meet and fulfill their deepest longings. But I have two observations that perhaps are more germane to reality. First, in each movie, at least one relationship has to end in order for the other to begin. In *Sleepless in Seattle* the Meg Ryan character is in a relationship with a guy that is likeable except he has a sinus problem. In *You've Got Mail*, the Tom Hanks character is in a relationship with a woman with a less-than-attractive personality. "What man would want to live with a narcissist?" the audience rationalizes. But upon more reflective analysis you can begin to see the problem. Other people's lives are affected here, and where one heart is hopeful, another is broken. But that doesn't make for a good romantic comedy, does it?

The second observation that would lead us into reality is how both movies end, one on top of the Empire State Building (they almost missed each other but they meet!) and the other in a New York City park. Both are just entering into the new and altered world of an established relationship and here's the rub: we don't see what happens, do we? What if the Meg Ryan character turns into being a closet narcissist and what if the Tom Hanks character developed sinus problems? My firm belief is that we really don't want to see what happens. We would rather live in the myth of finding the soulmate.

shift the focus from finding a soulmate to being a soulmate.

My parents met during World War II and were engaged three days later. My father shortly thereafter left for Alaska where he was stationed after he had developed malaria serving in the South Pacific. Six months later, my parents were married in a quiet ceremony at my father's Lutheran church in Ridgeville Corners, Ohio. They didn't know each other very well; my mother had been married before and had two children she brought into the marriage, and my father was thirty-one years old when he married. Not a classic formula for marital success. Forty-nine years later when my father died, he left a legacy of a marriage that withstood the challenges of being a blended family, the death of a two-year-old daughter, and the dysfunctions of their zany biological children. How did they do it? Well, two things come to mind immediately; the first was their faith in God and reliance on His power. The second was an indomitable willingness to do the hard work of a relationship. My parents weren't soulmates because they just were; they worked toward that end and persevered through difficult times.

Joe and Diane survived the challenge to their marriage. They did so by coming to grips with the fact that emotions are merely coincidental to a loving relationship. Joe finally realized that he needed to put effort into the relationship. He began by simply talking to her, and that evolved into being able to share his heart, his disappointments and frustrations included. And when he did this, he also discovered that what was created was something much more profound that what he had previously termed as "being in love." He sat in my office and articulated it this way: "Before, I just waited to feel a certain way and if the feeling didn't come, I didn't do anything in a loving manner. Now, I look for ways that I can show Diane that I love her, and I'm finding a much deeper emotional connection with her than I ever had imagined before. But it's a lot of work," he concluded, to which I heartily agreed.

Work is not drudgery in its essence. It certainly can become drudgery with the wrong attitudes and actions. But really, work is energy expended to reach a desired end. And it is also the realization that if that energy is not expended, nothing happens but decay. It takes work to be a soulmate.

being a soulmate requires self-focus not other-focus

In 1961, John F. Kennedy spoke some of the most well-known words in modern-day presidential history during his inaugural address. He said, "Ask not what your country can do for you; ask what you can do for your country." President Kennedy was on to something. And I honestly don't think that his sentiment is in high favor in our present-day world, although I don't think anyone would be eager to admit it. Our world today is all about unfairness and inequities and "not getting what I really deserve." The day of sacrifice and us honoring it are long gone. This attitude has reached into the fabric of our lives and has all but destroyed our ability to love unconditionally and to marry for a lifetime. The focus must be on what we can do to be obedient to God, not on what God can do for us. And consequently, the focus must be on what we can do for others, not on what others can do for us. The place to start is in our marriages.

The question that needs to be asked by every spouse is "What is it that my wife/husband legitimately needs from me today?" That focus is imperative to building intimacy in marriage. When my focus is on my needs, wants, and desires, I tend to lose sight of what it will take for me to be the spouse that will build intimacy into my marriage. One of the first couples that I counseled had incredible difficulty getting along and seeing eye to eye. The wife was perpetually angry with her husband and children, and her husband did everything he could to try to ameliorate her anger. Nothing seemed to work, until he said one day in session, "I think I might have stumbled onto something that works. I've noticed that if I can quit concentrating on how my wife is doing and responding to me, I can better focus on what I need to do to be healthy in our relationship and build oneness in our marriage. I've been too limited by judging my success on how she responds rather than on evaluating my response based on what God wants me to do regardless of her reaction." I told him I couldn't have said it better. Self-focus is not selfishness, it's the ability to do what needs to be done to fulfill our part of a loving and committed relationship. And I am not talking about co-dependency here either. Co-dependence has one goal in mind: make the other person happy. True love has quite another goal: I will focus on doing my part to love and speak truth to my spouse, regardless of his or her initial response.

being a soulmate is a lifelong process.

As I write this, I have been married thirty-five years. It sounds like a very long time but it doesn't feel long at all. I still feel the same inside and I still feel as if I'm learning what I need to do to be a loving and effective husband. Renee and I are soulmates, but we're still learning to be soulmates. When we stop learning, we'll stop being what we need to be for each other. And in addition, I don't think I'm always a very good soulmate to her, and if I neglect this too long, our relationship suffers—**she** suffers. So the day I stop learning how to love and be what I need to be is the day that the distancing and discomfort start, the day that could bring about the end of our relationship. And I'm not talking about divorce; I'm talking about emotional and relational isolation that leads to existing, not loving.

I recently went through a time of some diverse but serious medical problems. I tried to do this keeping my own counsel so as not concern Renee, but after three days (or in some cases three hours!) my resolve dwindled to the point of confession of fear. My wife fears just like me, and she doesn't enjoy the drama of illness, but she always rises to the occasion with love, concern, and comfort. She knows me inside out and knows what I need. It still makes me want to give her stuff! But most of all, it makes me want to love her better, to be there for her more during her times of difficulty. But every day for us both it's a decision, a decision to move toward not away. It's a decision to concentrate on what I can give, not what I can get. And you know what? I end up agreeing with the concluding line in a Beatles' song on their *Abbey Road* album: "And in the end, the love you take is equal to the love you make." Actually, now that I think about it, I take far more than I deserve, thanks to the graciousness of God and the gift of a loving wife.

So when it comes to soulmates, instead of focusing on finding one, I would strongly suggest you be a soulmate to the spouse you already have. It's the only healthy path to intimacy that I know.

chapter 12

don't go home
for christmas

*But at the beginning of creation God "made
them male and female." "For this reason a man
will leave his father and mother, and be united
to his wife, and the two shall become one flesh"...
Therefore what God has joined together,
let no one separate.*

MARK 10:6-9 NIV

A couple disclaimers are in order before diving into this chapter. First, I am writing this between Christmas and New Year's Day. I love Christmas more than any other time of the year. It is replete with many positive memories, and our family still adheres to several rituals that make this time of the year complete. We still do Christmas stockings, read the Christmas story before opening gifts on Christmas morning (which is the only biblical time to open presents!), and I watch *It's a Wonderful Life* from beginning to end during Christmas season. I usually watch it alone and I always cry at the end. So, Renee and I spent the twenty-fifth with my daughter and her husband and children. We thoroughly enjoyed the time and trust that my daughter did as well. Nothing like a three-year-old grandson to liven up the festivities! Second, I look forward to the holidays and sincerely hope that we spend many more holidays together with my adult children and their families. With that being said, my sincere advice to married couples is don't go home for Christmas.

With the exception of Easter, Christmas is the most cherished of all days for Christians and it without a doubt is the most nostalgic and emotion-packed of all the holidays. If you want people to share some of their most impactful experiences in life, Christmas is a great place to start. As a therapist I never fail to hear a client's heart-felt response to the day which commemorates Jesus' birth. The scale ranges from "I am a Christmas nut" to "I cannot stand Christmas," and all the variations in between. The weeks leading up to and away from Christmas are some of the busiest for counselors. I suppose there are more sophisticated analyses as to why, but my unscientific opinion is people go into Christmas with great hopes and anticipation but come out of the holidays with disappointment and many times disillusionment. The good news about Christmas is that families get together. The bad news about Christmas is that it exacerbates family dysfunction! But this chapter isn't so much about Christmas; it's about the emotional dynamics swirling around our families of origin. Christmas just happens to be one of the times when those dynamics are most keenly felt. All spouses bring their families and their family history into their marriages. It borders on the simplistic to say that our parents have had a profound effect on our lives, were the primary shapers of our identity, and serve as our models as to how husbands and wives should function in a marriage.

Chad and Bonnie were a young couple I counseled some years ago, specifically to deal with anxiety they had about their holiday plans. Both were dreading the impending family time, and for different reasons. Chad loathed the false intimacy that came during this time of the year. His family had been close growing up, but his parents were attached to his life in an unhealthy way and he had done his best to distance himself from their over-involvement and unhealthy expectations. His mother relied a bit too much on her relationship with her son for her own emotional well-being, and would use the time to make a fuss over Chad and go out of her way to meet his every need. She wanted him to return the attention and was always a bit disappointed when her expectations weren't met. She silently blamed Bonnie for the distance she felt from her son. Chad's father had relied on him to keep Chad's mother happy, neglecting his own responsibilities in the marriage. So Chad's father would make statements like, "Your mother could use some encouragement," or "It wouldn't hurt you to spend a little time with your Mom." Holiday meals were a charade, a family pretending everything was as it should be relationally, and issues that really mattered were swept under the rug and never dealt with.

Bonnie, on the other hand, had grown up in a family that had little emotional connection. Her holiday experience was a grim reminder that no one in her family loved unconditionally. Visits home ended up being endurance contests, and many times they left her parent's home earlier than expected. When I gave them my "don't go home for Christmas" advice, they looked at me with alarm. "My mother will be so upset she won't speak to me for months!" Chad said. "Maybe that wouldn't be such a bad thing," Bonnie responded. You didn't have to be a therapist to hear the irony in her voice.

"What would be the harm, ultimately, if you both decided that you just wanted to do Christmas on your own?" I asked. Chad and Bonnie looked at each other as if the thought had never occurred to them. Come to think of it, I don't think it actually ever had.

"That would be an experience neither of us has ever had," Bonnie said.

We talked through why spending Christmas as a couple with no extended family obligations might be a good change of pace. They agreed with the concept, but didn't want the emotional response they would get from both sets of parents.

"Why do your parents still control your life?" I asked Chad.

"They don't control my life," he protested, but his answer lacked conviction and his answer was accompanied by his wife's rolling eyes.

"They do too," she responded, "and you are always trying to make sure you're doing everything they want you to do so they'll continue to think of you as their 'sweet little Chad.'"

The passage at the beginning of this chapter is the classic verse concerning marriage in Scripture. A man must leave his parents in order for him to be united with his wife in a healthy manner. My wife's mother set an important boundary when Renee told her we were engaged. After the initial excitement, my mother-in-law looked at her daughter seriously and said, "I want you to know I love you very much, but once you're married you cannot come home again." Renee was initially confused, but her mother explained that marriage would at times be difficult, and the only way to work through those difficulties healthily is to stay with the spouse God has given you and resolve the conflict. Running home to mother was not an option. It was good advice because it gave us the opportunity to work through our issues without the undue temptation of being able to even temporarily leave the marriage.

Let me suggest five family-of-origin traps that interfere with a couple's growing closer together and putting each other first:

1. **inadequate launching**: I always get a kick out of the word "launching" to describe the time when adult children leave their childhood home to go live in the real world. Our culture has become increasingly indulgent to adult children, and there has been more of a resistance to letting adult children be on their own. Even when adult children leave, all too often they return to their parents' home because of personal or financial reasons. I affectionately call these children "baby boomerangers." Unhealthy ties to parents often allow an adult child to make poor personal decisions, and if they are married it can allow them to make poor relational decisions as well.

Ed and Christa had been married one year when Ed was transferred to a job 500 miles away from Christa's parents. Up to that point, they had lived only minutes away, and Christa would see her mother up to five times a week.

Christa was an only child, and the move was quite traumatic for her and her mother. During the first month in their new location, she was on the phone with her mother daily, and as more time passed, Ed and Christa began to have more and more conflict which caused their marriage to suffer greatly. Ed's job became more and more demanding, and Christa's new job was not satisfying to her at all. Ed suggested she do more schooling, and she finally agreed. But the distance between them grew greater and greater. Sixteen months after their transition, Ed came home to an empty house. Without any warning, Christa had packed her bags and gone home to see her parents. "Marriage to you is just too hard," read her note. "I don't think that you need me like my mother needs me, and I know I'll be happier at home." Even though her initial note said that it would be a temporary separation, Christa eventually filed for divorce. Ed was devastated.

Ed and Christa's story is not uncommon. Even though they had some difficult obstacles to overcome, I'm convinced they could have worked them through had Christa stayed. But she had not been totally released by her mother—there was no "You cannot come home" message that was communicated to her. Instead, her mother was complicit in her abandoning her marriage. Christa's mother was happy because Christa was her life, due to an emotionless marriage with Christa's father. It was easier for Christa to go home and be with her mother who doted on her, as opposed to staying in a marriage that required work and change.

2. **over-dependence on parents**: When I first began counseling, a young couple (early twenties) scheduled to see me for marital therapy. They had two young

children and the emotional and financial strains that came along with their family situation. They began to relate their story to me, and since I already knew that their parents were paying for the therapy, and I asked them about their relationship with them. "Oh, my parents are really great," said the husband. "They help with the kids' pre-K and pay our auto insurance." "And my parents are wonderful too," the wife joined in, "they help with our rent and pay half our expenses for groceries." My initial thought was to ask where I could find parents like that, or even if their parents would adopt me! I certainly could have used the help financially. But the next question I asked was more to the point: "And what do you pay your parents in return?"

Both spouses looked down and were silent for about thirty seconds. Finally the wife simply said, "Too much." The parents, even though I'm sure they were well-meaning, used their financial leverage to purchase an inordinate amount of influence in the lives of their children and grandchildren too. How was this couple to say no to two sets of parents who were so supportive? But the wife's mother expected her to be at her beck and call, and the husband's father who was also his boss, regularly expected him to go above and beyond what he expected his other employees to do. And they didn't dare go against their suggestions as to the raising of their children. Too much, indeed.

Well-meaning parents are all too often guilty of protecting their adult children from the pain of bad choices, when that pain is the tutor that has the best chance of building the experience and character their children need to make better decisions down the road. Too much dependence on parents short-circuits the learning process that needs to take place to bring maturity to the marriage relationship. While we love giving to our children, Renee and I always measure our giving against the risk of enabling. As a parent of adult children, I feel I need to be a safety net, not a hammock.

3. attempting to repair the irreparable: One of my gifts (I believe) is the gift of being positive. I believe that almost anyone can change, be healed, and decide to grow. But the word "almost" leads to my greatest weakness. I can become unrealistically optimistic about a person or a relationship's ability to heal. And there are some parent-child relationships that fall into this category.

Chad's mother was not a healthy person. His parents were in a stable but unhealthy marriage, and Chad was made responsible for her happiness. Chad's brother handled their mother's unhappiness by moving to the opposite coast, but Chad felt that he still could help make his mother happy.

This situation came to a head the next Christmas Chad and Bonnie spent with his parents. I asked him to limit his time with his family and to focus on talking with his father more than his mother. When Christmas Day came, and he followed through on this, his mother became increasingly agitated and unhappy. His father all but physically pushed Chad to be present for his mother, but he was diligent in focusing on his father.

Christmas turned out to be a bust—tears, awkward silences, and premature departures. Chad came in after Christmas stressed and in despair. "What do I do?" he asked in desperation. "What is your goal in your relationship with your mother?" I responded. He was perplexed at the question. "Do you have to have goals in order to relate to your parents? Aren't you just supposed to be there and love them?"

"Loving them is a good thing," I responded, "but I think you need to take a fresh look at what you need in order to have a healthy relationship with your mother, and then set boundaries to accomplish it. For right now, it's obvious your mother is displeased with your attempts to meet her needs and to now be there for your father as well as her, so I would suggest you say to your mother something like, 'Mom, you obviously are displeased with my desire to spend time with my father and from what I saw this last Christmas it causes you hurt. So, I've decided that we won't be coming for Christmas, because I know how much sadness it will cause you if I don't spend the bulk of my time with you on such a special day.' Don't go home for Christmas," I said.

"That will make her furious," Chad said, trying to comprehend the thought of standing up to his mother. "I'm sure you're right," I told him, "but if you don't stop trying to fix your mother, you will cause yourself and your marriage great stress and potentially great harm." Chad pondered my advice, talked about it with Bonnie and most importantly prayed about it before deciding that he would do what I suggested

When I did a follow-up with Chad after Christmas, I asked him what he finally decided. "Well, the conclusion I came to is that I will never be able to fix my mother. I will continue to set boundaries to let her know what it will take for me to have a healthy relationship with her, but I allowed her to decide whether or not she wanted me to come for Christmas, given the fact that I was going spend a limited amount of time with them and focus primarily on my relationship with my father. She decided that she would rather not see me, so we didn't go." "How did you do?" I asked. "It was tough going into the day, but to be honest, it was the best Christmas I've ever had." Chad discovered that you cannot fix your parents; you can just fix yourself and provide an environment to allow your parent to grow as well.

4. parenting your parents: Whenever I am able to do something for my children for which they thank me, my joking response is, "Just remember me when I'm old and be there to wipe the drool from my mouth." I thought this remarkably clever ten years ago, but I've noticed lately that I "joke" a bit more seriously about growing old. Now I don't want to be a burden to my children and am planning accordingly. But I realize, and I suppose they do as well, that the day might come when they need to be a bit more parental with me in a caretaking role. That being said, I strongly believe that children should not parent their parents.

Annie had been married for three years when she and her husband Hal came to see me. Among the rough spots in their marriage was the fact that Annie felt responsible to make sure that her parents were functioning well. I thought initially that what she was doing was loving and admirable. She would visit her parents' home almost once a day and prepare meals for them on a regular basis. I then asked her parents' age and she said just past sixty for both of them. "Are they in good health?" I asked. "Very good, thank the Lord," Annie responded, "and I hope they continue that way for decades to come." I asked Hal what he thought of her involvement in her parents' lives and without hesitation he said he didn't like it at all. With that, Annie teared up and said, "This is why we have problems! Hal doesn't like the way I love my parents!" I asked her why she spent so much time with her folks, and she said "I just like taking care of them. It seems like that's always been my role and it just comes natural."

Annie's problem was that her over-involvement with her parents was having a detrimental effect on her marriage. Her parents had grown to expect her to be their caretaker, and she received a good portion of her affirmation from that role. We began to work through what would be a more healthy set of boundaries given that her parents were relatively young and more than capable of caring for themselves. Annie explained to them that her involvement in their lives was compromising her marriage, and even though this was difficult news to digest for her folks, to their credit they came to understand and were in agreement to change their expectations.

It's also interesting to me that I've seen this situation

with just as many men as women. In fact, men tend to be the more zealous in parenting, the primary fear being that if they don't take care of their parents, then something bad will happen and they'll feel responsible. My advice is always not to parent your parents.

5. attempting to please: All good children want to please their parents. At least that is what our culture and the sociologists tell us. Certainly parental approval is a prime factor in how we grow morally, psychologically, and relationally. And it is not unusual to take this willingness to please into adulthood. Many of my clients have had troubled and unhealthy relationships with their parents, and their strategy to deal with this reality revolved around being "good" so their parents would not get angry and negative. This is particularly true in families where one or both parents have addictions or a serious emotional illness. Many times children will attempt to be perfect in order to make their home environment more pleasant and less negative. If this is indeed the case, then it is not unusual at all for the child to take this propensity into his or her adult years.

Bonnie, Chad's wife, was an only child and was the emotional caretaker for her mother. Her father was an alcoholic and could not hold down a job. Bonnie's mother worked two jobs and devoted her life to her own personal survival. No emotional support was offered Bonnie, and she had to learn to fend for herself at an early age. But that didn't stop her from wanting to please her parents and one day getting the love she had always desired from one or both of them.

As Chad and Bonnie talked through their situation, it became evident to me that Bonnie was trying to keep her parents happy as well as her husband. She would regularly send money when they needed it and would help them make basic decisions such as where they would live and how to handle their limited finances. But even though they took all of this from her without a second thought, they never communicated any appreciation in return, let alone love. She began to see that this situation wasn't going to get better, and took steps to make sure that her mother understood that she would need to create a little space between her and her daughter and grandchildren. Bonnie explained to her parents that she felt used and tolerated, and because of this reality, she wouldn't be spending time with them until they addressed the dysfunction in their relationship. Her parents responded with hurt and anger, but Bonnie didn't back down. She also did not go home for Christmas!

The key to making sure that a spouse's family of origin does not have an undue influence on the marriage is rooted in Mark 10:6-9 (NIV). The leaving is the prerequisite to the uniting, which allows a couple to become one flesh. Leaving must be done appropriately, with honor and respect. And parents of adult children must be open and willing to weigh in with advice and help when it is asked for and warranted. But honoring a parent and being obedient to a parent are two different categories. They certainly overlap when a child is not in his or her majority, but the requirement of obedience ceases when the child becomes an adult. Honor, however, must continue throughout the rest of the relationship, unless there are severe circumstantial issues such as abuse or abject neglect. But boundaries must be put in place to make sure that the proper attention is given to the most important relationship in the family: the marriage. Appropriate boundaries must be established so there is no undue influence from parents on their married children.

I am enthusiastic about extended family relationships. One of the joys of extended families is the involvement of the grandparents and great-grandparents in the lives of the children. Open lines of communication and the ability to resolve differences remain important so as to allow those grandparents to enjoy the blessing of the involvement in the lives of their children and grandchildren. My admonition to all married couples is to do nothing with your families of origin out of begrudging obligation, or to try to help when it is not your role to help. What is mandatory at these times is a dialogue between adult children and parents that will establish and clarify roles and expectations. When family members are willing to go into this dialogue, I believe that good outcomes are the result. When they are not, you will be forced back to a sense of duty, rather than joyful community. And when you are feeling that sense of dreaded duty, my advice remains the same: don't go home for Christmas!

[epilogue]

"Two are better than one, because they have a good return for their labor. For if either of them falls, the one will lift up his companion. But woe to the one who falls when there is not another to lift him up... And if one can overpower him who is alone, two can resist him. A cord of three strands is not quickly torn apart."
ECCLESIASTES 4:9, 10, 12 NASB

At the time of writing this epilogue, I am recovering from open-heart surgery. I knew most of my adult life that eventually I would have to have my aortic valve replaced, but I was never quite prepared for the vulnerabilities that surgery would bring. The time for surgery came somewhat unexpectedly, just as I was wrapping up this book. Major surgery has a way of getting your attention, reminding you or your mortality, and helping you evaluate what's really important. For me, experiencing this surgery reminded me that my relationship with God, my family, and my wife, Renee, are the most important things in my life.

Thanks to my very capable doctors, nurses, and caring friends and family, I made it through with flying colors. But my wife Renee was the one who shouldered the majority of the burden emotionally and physically during the toughest part of recovery. We learned a lot about one another and the strength of our marriage through the numerous consults with doctors, countless walks, conversations, evaluations, and mutual frustrations. We even made a trip to our local fire station to check out my BP and

EKG—that was fun!

I was struck by the consistency of a love—one that cares deeply, strongly, and with great compassion—that has lasted three and a half decades. Those of you who have been through health situations such as these already know the stress and trauma they can cause. But what I was able to enjoy this past month is a marriage that has been deeply rooted in mutual commitment. I have been continually humbled by the fact that my wife loves me sacrificially, and in turn, it makes me want to love her back all the more. This was a physical struggle and also a spiritual one, but whatever the hardship, Renee (and sometimes me, too!) was able to regain perspective, and we travelled this journey together seeking to love each other better each day.

After reading this book, you may have started to realize that when it comes to putting your marriage on the right track, all is not as it first appears. In fact, our initial instincts are not always the best ones. Taking time to stop and rethink our instinctive responses can go a long way to making marriage healthier, more enjoyable, and sustainable.

To embody the upside down marriage approach to have a right side up marriage, it is important to focus on humility, not on winning the issue. In fact, it takes each individual dealing with their own lives first, rather than blaming their spouse, to really thrive. Too many marriages end up in capsized because one or both spouses don't take responsibility for their own issues.

[acknowledgments]

This book is the result of a confluence of people and events, and I am grateful to those whose encouragement and enthusiasm were critical in the creation of this work. First of all, thanks to Dennis Rainey who launched this voyage with the simple question, "So, when are you going to write your book?" Dennis, your follow-up and encouragement were the catalyst to get me started. Second, thanks to my son, Chris, who believed in me enough to be my initial editor and most exquisite critic. Your input and enthusiasm were an essential piece in this literary puzzle. Third, thanks to Mark Russell, my publisher, and all the folks at Russell Media. You were with me each step of the way, always cheerleading and making the journey exciting and fun.

Countless friends were also instrumental in their assistance. The crew I am privileged to work with at Charis Counseling was a source of wisdom and focus. Thanks Melissa, Julia, Tim, Alexis and Laura… you're the best. My tennis buddies (the Gang of Six) were merciless in their prodding to get this project done. Thanks Bob, Skeeter, Alan, Elden, and Perry. It's done now!

Thanks to my wife, Renee, whose statement, "I like it," upon reading the first three chapters of my book was music to my ears and motivation to my soul. Thanks for standing with me and never complaining about the time it took to write this book. It's been a thirty-six year journey, babe, and it's been a great one! Words cannot express what you mean to me…

Thanks to my wonderful clients, the men and women who are

brave enough to tackle the important stuff. You are a continual source of inspiration and encouragement to me. I've learned far more from you than you could ever learn from me. It's a privilege to know you and to be able to be a small part of your story. Without you this book could never have been written.

Thanks to my daughter Beth for her constant encouragement and support. Chris and Beth, you are the best!

Finally, "May the God of peace, who through the blood of the eternal covenant brought back from the dead our Lord Jesus, that great Shepherd of the sheep, equip you with everything good for doing his will, and may he work in us what is pleasing to him, through Jesus Christ, to whom be glory for ever and ever. Amen." Hebrews 13: 20, 21 (NIV)

[what i'd like to change to make my marriage better]

_____

_____

_____

_____

_____

_____

_____

_____

_____

_____

_____

_____

_____

_____

_____

[things God is showing me about us]

[things God is showing me about our marriage]

[ten blessings my spouse is to me]

Visit Russell Media for our latest offerings:

www.russell-media.com